INK and ASHES

DISCLAIMER

Copyright © 2025 by Dexton Jack Simic
First published in 2025
All rights reserved.

Published by **Storyline House Publishing**
www.storylinehouse.com

This poetry collection is a work of creative expression. Unless explicitly stated, all characters, events, and scenarios are fictional and are not intended to reference real individuals, events, or places. Reader discretion is advised, as some content may include themes that are sensitive or triggering to certain audiences. All content is protected under copyright law. Unauthorised reproduction, distribution, or use of this material without prior written consent is strictly prohibited.

No part of this book may be reproduced, stored in, or transmitted in any form or by any means — electronic, mechanical, photocopying, recording, or otherwise — without prior written permission from the publisher, except for brief quotations (under 10%) used in reviews, articles, or for other non-commercial purposes as permitted under copyright law.

Publisher: Storyline House Publishing
Publishing Support and Production Oversight: Sarah Jayd
Author: Dexton Jack Simic
ISBN: 978-1-7644258-0-3
For distribution or rights inquiries: hello@storylinehouse.com

About Storyline House Publishing: *An independent publishing house dedicated to supporting writers and authors on their self-publishing journey. We believe every storyteller deserves the tools, guidance, and confidence to bring their book to life. From concept to completion, we provide high-touch support, creative direction, and professional expertise, empowering authors to publish independently while retaining full ownership of their work.*

Our mission is simple: *To make self-publishing easier, more accessible, and deeply rewarding – so every story finds its voice and every author leaves a legacy.*

www.storylinehouse.com

SYNOPSIS

In a world that often demands perfection, we find ourselves yearning for authenticity. This book is an invitation to embark on a transformative journey – a journey that delves deep into the heart of vulnerability and the power of shared experiences. Here, I lay bare my own struggles, triumphs, and the myriad emotions that accompany the human experience.

As I share my story, I hope to create a space where we can all connect, reflect, and grow together. This is not just my journey; it is ours. Through candid reflections and heartfelt insights, we will explore the complexities of mental health and the challenges life throws our way.

Join me as we navigate the highs and lows, the light and the shadows, and discover the strength that lies in our shared humanity. Together, we can foster understanding, support one another, and ultimately help those who may be silently battling their own demons. Let's embrace the rawness of life and cultivate a community of compassion and resilience. Welcome to a journey of healing, growth, and connection.

DEDICATION

This book is dedicated to you, my beautiful daughter, the light that pierced through my darkest nights. You may never fully understand the depth of your impact on my journey, but I hope these words convey the gratitude that swells within me. You were my beacon when the shadows loomed large, a gentle reminder that even in the depths of despair, love can ignite the spark of hope.

Every page of this book is infused with the essence of your unwavering support and the strength you unknowingly bestowed upon me. It was your laughter that echoed in my mind during the moments I felt most alone, your belief in me that propelled me forward when I wanted to retreat into the safety of my own darkness. You inspired me to confront my demons, to wrestle with the pain that had long been my companion, and to emerge, scarred yet resilient, on the other side.

In the quiet moments of reflection, I often think of the countless times you stood by me, your presence a soothing balm to my troubled soul. You taught me that vulnerability is not a weakness but a profound strength, a bridge that connects us to one another. It is through your love that I found the courage to share my story, to peel back the layers of hurt and reveal the raw, unfiltered truth of my existence.

As I pen these words, I am reminded that healing is not a solitary journey; it is a tapestry woven with the threads of connection, compassion, and shared experience. This book is a testament to the battles fought and the victories won, all inspired by you. May it serve as a reminder that even in our darkest moments, we are never truly alone. Thank you for being my guiding star, for believing in me when I struggled to believe in myself. This is for you, and for everyone who has ever fought their own battle in silence. Together, we rise.

DEDICATION

To my beloved Mum,

In the quiet corners of my heart, where words often tremble to take form, you reside as the most profound inspiration. You are the gentle whisper that ignited the spark of poetry within me, the guiding light that illuminated the path of my soul. With every line I write, I feel your love wrapping around me like a warm embrace, reminding me that I am never alone in this vast universe.

You taught me the meaning of unconditional love, a love that knows no bounds, that forgives without hesitation, and that nurtures without expectation. You showed me how to see beauty in the mundane, how to find strength in vulnerability, and how to weave my emotions into verses that resonate with the very essence of humanity. Your laughter was my favourite melody, your tears my deepest sorrow, and your dreams the canvas upon which I painted my own.

You were my entire world, the heartbeat of my existence, and the reason I dared to dream. In your eyes, I found my worth; in your arms, I discovered safety; and in your spirit, I learned to soar. Now, as I pen these words, I am acutely aware of the void your absence has left, a chasm that echoes with the memories of your love.

This book is not just a collection of poems; it is a testament to you, a tribute to the woman who shaped my very being. Each word is a fragment of my heart, a reflection of the lessons you imparted, and a promise to carry your legacy forward.

Thank you for being my muse, my anchor, and my guiding star. I hope to honour you with every syllable, to make you proud in ways that words can scarcely capture. Though you may no longer walk beside me, your spirit dances in every line, and your love will forever be the ink that fills my pages.

Pocivaj sa anđelima majko moja.

For Dr Merima Isakovic

In the depths of my darkest nights, you held a lantern to my soul, guiding me through the shadows.

Your unwavering belief in my worth breathed life into my shattered spirit.

Thank you for teaching me that healing is not just a journey, but a profound act of love.

I am forever grateful for your light in my life.

MY MUM'S TESTIMONY

I HAVE NOTHING TO REGRET

If I'm lucky enough to grow old one day and count the wrinkles on my face, I will smile, place my hand on my heart, let a tear fall and say: I gave my all so that everyone I love could feel happiness and have a beautiful life embraced by my love... I have nothing to regret... because I have never told to any of them "I can't" or "I won't." I answered every call and I was always where they needed me.

I will caress every pore on my face and feel proud... I will not be ashamed, for each one holds a valuable life story that will be written by my own hand as a keepsake for those who are just beginning their lives.

NEMAM SE ZBOG ČEGA KAJATI

Ako budem imala sreće da ostarim jednoga dana i zbrojim bore na svome licu, nasmiješit ću se, staviti ruku na srce, pustiti suzu i reći: Dala sam sve od sebe da svi koje volim osjete sreću i da im uz mene bude lijepo... Nemam se zbog čega kajati...jer nikada nikome od njih nisam rekla ne mogu i neću. Na svaki poziv sam se odazvala i bila na mjestu na kojem su me trebali.

Pomilovat ću svaku poru na svome licu i biti ponosna...neću se sramiti, svaka od njih nosi po jednu vrijednu životnu priču koja će biti ispisana mojom rukom za uspomenu onima, koji tek počinju živjeti...

ABOUT THE AUTHOR

DEXTON JACK SIMIC

I was born on September 19, 1984, in Zadar, Croatia, into a world divided by war and faith. My childhood was anything but innocent – haunted by violence, bullying, and the devastating loss of my best friend. In 1995, my family fled to Serbia, and by 1997 we found ourselves in Perth, Australia, where I struggled to learn a new language and navigate a life that felt foreign.

In 2004, I became a parent, and my daughter became my anchor in the storm. But even motherhood came with its own battles – performing CPR on her in 2005 tested my strength in ways I never imagined. I poured my pain into service, spending five years with the Northern Territory Emergency Service, including work during the Queensland floods.

My journey has been marked by heartbreak: domestic violence, miscarriages, homelessness, addiction, and assaults that pushed me to the edge of survival. In 2017, I began my transition, a step toward living my truth, though it cost me the acceptance of many I loved. Addiction nearly claimed my life, and there were times I welcomed the end. But the doctors who revived me with a defibrillator reminded me that my story wasn't finished.

In 2023, I started over in Tamworth, NSW. Today, I stand 721 days sober, proof that even the darkest paths can lead to light. Poetry became my lifeline, turning pain into purpose. My story is one of survival, resilience, and rebirth – a reminder that no matter how many times we fall, we can rise again.

CONTENTS

In the Shadow of Your Absence	06
Whispers of Absence	08
Resilience in Shadows	10
In the Silence of His Cot	12
A Daughter's Blessing	14
A Mother's Lament	16
The Tapestry of Trials	18
When Love Transforms: A Journey of Hearts	20
To the Heart That Bore Us	22
Forever 22	24
Whispers in the Shadows	26
Echoes of the Unseen	28
A Whisper in the Abyss	30
Resurrection of Shadows	32
Welcome to My Truth	34
A Dreamer's Journey	36
Eight Years of Becoming	38
In Shadows Deep	40
Whispers in the Dark	42
Eclipsed by You	44
Shattered Reflections	46
Whispers in the Wind	48
Silent Symphony	50
The Solitary Path	52
Echoes of a Dreamer	54
From Shadows to Light: A Journey of Truth	56
Whispers of Innocence	58
Unveiling the Mirror	60
Shattered Dreams	62
For Hamish, My Heart's Whisper	64
The Weight of Their Dreams	66
In the Shadow of My Heart	68

CONTENTS

The Grave I Dig	70
In Search of a Heartbeat	72
Two Years in the Abyss	74
To My Beautiful Daughter	76
To Those Battling the Black Dog	78
A Tribute to Elspeth Cook	80
In the Echo of a Crowd	82
In the Shadow of Their Love	84
Shattered Whispers	86
Echoes of the Abyss	88
Echoes of Worthlessness	90
The Battle Within	92
Unseen Beauty	94
Awakening the Soul	96
In the Depths of Shadow	98
Let Me Be Clear	100
Paradox of the Heart	102
Sanctuary of Sweat	104
What If	106
The Cost of Shadows: A Journey to Light	108
Unapologetically Me: A Symphony of One	110
Chapters of Strength	112
To My Princess, My Light	114
Echoes of Connection	116
Inside You, the World	118
A Mother's Heart	120
From Shadows to Light	122
One Life	124
A Glimpse of Blue	126
Remember	128
Fragments of a Shattered Soul	130
The Echo of Loss	132
In the Echoes of a Child's Heart	134

CONTENTS

The Weight of Shadows — 136
Life's Cruel Curriculum — 138
Resilient Heart — 140
In the Mirror of Our Hearts — 142
The Price of Shadows — 144
Home in the Heart:
A Journey to Acceptance — 146
From Ashes to Wings — 148
Fractured Chains — 150
Shadows of Jack — 152
Echoes of Absence — 154
From Ashes to Strength — 156
Dear Family, — 158
Echoes of a Shattered Dream — 160
In the Silence of War — 162
In the Heart of the Storm — 164
Resilient Heart — 166
Behind the Mask — 168
In Shadows We Dwell — 170
Fragmented Echoes — 172
The Weight of Choices — 174
In the Beautiful Mess — 176
The Legacy of a Big Kid — 178
Resurrection of the Silent — 180
Whispers of the Unbound — 182
When Bad Things End — 184
The Keeper of Secrets — 186
In the Depths of Shadows — 188
In the Quiet of Shadows — 190
Whispers of the Silent Storm — 192
Echoes of Emptiness — 194
Ephemeral Echoes — 196

CONTENTS

Hollow Echoes \ **198**
Whispers of the Abyss \ **200**
Shadows of the Heart \ **202**
The Mask I Wear \ **204**
The Depths of My Heart \ **206**
The Weight of Being Real \ **208**
From Shadows to Strength: A Journey Reborn \ **210**
Ink and Ashes \ **214**
Kill Them with Success \ **216**
Echoes of the Soul \ **218**
Whispers of the Forgotten \ **220**
In the Shadow of Awakening \ **222**
The Weight of Unseen Waters \ **224**
The Mirror of Despair \ **226**
Echoes of Resilience \ **228**
Whispers of Strength \ **230**
Threads of Endurance \ **232**
Echoes of the Forgotten \ **234**
To My Little Girl \ **236**
Whispers of Jack \ **238**
In the Shadows of Ink \ **240**
Three Years Without You \ **242**
In the Weight of Absence \ **244**
Echoes of Absence \ **246**
A Birthday in Heaven \ **248**
Whispers of a Grandmother's Heart \ **250**
In the Echo of Your Heart \ **252**
Six Months Without You \ **254**
A Promise in the Ashes \ **256**
The Fire Within \ **258**
In the Quiet of Your Care \ **260**
To Rose, My Guiding Light \ **262**

In the Shadow of Your Absence

In the quiet corners of my heart,
Where shadows linger, and memories start,
You were the light, my steadfast flame,
In a world that turned, you called my name.

When others faltered, when others fled,
You stood beside me, where angels tread.
With arms wide open, you held my fears,
You wiped away my sorrowful tears.

You saw the truth in my tangled soul,
Accepted my flaws, made me feel whole.
In your embrace, I learned to believe,
In the power of love, in the strength to grieve.

But now the silence is deafening, deep,
In the void of your absence, I struggle to keep
The pieces of me that you nurtured with care,
How do I walk on when you're no longer there?

Your guiding hand, a compass so true,
Now I wander lost, in a world without you.
Each step feels heavy, each breath a fight,
In the shadow of your love, I search for the light.

How do I carry the lessons you taught,
When the warmth of your presence is all that I sought?
Unconditional love, a gift from your heart,
Now feels like a puzzle, a world torn apart.
I long for your laughter, your gentle embrace,
The way you would smile, the light on your face.
In dreams, you return, a whisper, a sigh,
But morning awakens, and I'm left to cry.

So here I stand, with a heart full of ache,
A soul that is shattered, a spirit that breaks.
Yet in every tear, in each sorrowful song,
I'll carry your love, where I truly belong.

For though you have left, your essence remains,
In the love that you gave, in the joy and the pains.
I'll honour your memory, I'll cherish your name,
In the depths of my heart, you'll forever be the same.

So guide me, dear mother, from realms up above,
In the silence, I'll listen, I'll feel your love.
And though I may stumble, and though I may fall,
Your spirit will lift me, your love conquers all.

Whispers of Absence

In the quiet corners of a dim-lit room,
Where shadows dance with the scent of perfume,
I sit with the echoes of laughter long gone,
A heart heavy laden, a spirit withdrawn.

Twenty years, a lifetime, a blink of an eye,
Yet here I remain, with questions that cry:
Where did you wander, my sweet, precious child?
In the silence between us, I feel so reviled.

I trace the old photos, your smile shining bright,
A flicker of joy in the depths of the night.
But time has a way of unravelling threads,
And love, once a river, now trickles instead.

I remember the moments, the dreams that we shared,
The hopes that I nurtured, the love that we bared.
But distance has grown like a chasm so wide,
And I'm left with the memories, the tears that I hide.

Do you think of me, love, in your bustling days?
Or am I a ghost in your vibrant maze?
I reach for the phone, but my courage will wane,
What words could I muster to bridge all this pain?

I long for your laughter, your voice in the air,
To feel your embrace, to know that you care.
But silence is heavy, a weight on my chest,
A mother's heart breaking, a soul in unrest.

I send you my wishes on whispers of wind,
In hopes that you'll hear me, that we can begin
To mend what is broken, to heal what is torn,
To find our way back, to the love we once worn.

So here I will wait, in the stillness of night,
With a heart full of longing, a flicker of light.
For love knows no distance, no time can erase,
The bond that we share, the warmth of your grace.

And if you should stumble upon thoughts of the past,
Know that my love for you is steadfast, it lasts.
Though estranged, though apart, you're forever my own,
In the depths of my heart, you'll never be alone.

Resilience in Shadows

In the stillness of night, when the world felt so cold,
I wandered through darkness, my heart growing old.
A whisper of silence, a scream in my mind,
In the depths of despair, I thought peace I would find.

The weight of my sorrow, a burden so deep,
A chasm of anguish where hope dared not creep.
Each heartbeat a reminder of battles I'd fought,
In the depths of my being, I felt so distraught.

I stood on the edge, where the shadows entwined,
With a heart full of pain and a soul left behind.
The call of the void, a siren's sweet song,
In that moment of weakness, I felt I belonged.

But then came the light, in a flash and a blur,
Doctors and voices, a frantic stir.
They pulled me from darkness, from the brink of my end,
With hands that were steady, they fought to defend.

I felt the sharp pain, the struggle, the fight,
As they brought me back from the depths of the night.
A body once broken, now tethered to breath,
In the chaos of life, I was kissed by death.

Yet here I stand, a survivor reborn,
With scars that remind me of battles I've worn.
Each tear that I shed, each moment of strife,
A testament woven into the fabric of life.

I carry the weight of the pain that I knew,
But I also hold hope, a light breaking through.
For in the abyss, I found strength to survive,
A flicker of courage that helps me to thrive.

So I honour the struggle, the darkness I faced,
And the hands that reached out, the love that embraced.
Though shadows may linger, I choose to stand tall,
A survivor, a warrior, I rise through it all.

In the Silence of His Cot

In the quiet of the night, where shadows softly creep,
A mother's heart is heavy, in memories she weeps.
Two years of laughter stolen, like whispers in the breeze,
A baby boy named Zoran, now resting 'neath the trees.

I never held you, brother, never felt your tiny hand,
Yet in the depths of longing, I feel you understand.
Your laughter echoes softly, a melody so sweet,
In dreams, I see you dancing, your little heart's heartbeat.

Your cot stands still and empty, a shrine of what could be,
With clothes untouched, still folded, a testament to thee.
I picture you in sunlight, arms raised to the sky,
"Doviđenja" softly playing, as you twirl and fly.

Oh, how my mother mourns you, her baby boy, her light,
Each tear a silent story, each sigh a whispered night.
She cradles all the moments, the dreams that slipped away,
In every corner of her heart, you forever will stay.

I feel your spirit near me, in the rustle of the leaves,
In the laughter of the children, in the warmth of summer eves.
Though time may steal the present, and shadows may obscure,
The bond we share, dear Zoran, is a love that will endure.

So here I stand, a witness, to the love that never fades,
To the joy and to the sorrow, in the memories we've made.
Though I never met you, brother, your essence fills the air,
In the dance of life and longing, I know you're always there.

In the silence of your cot, where dreams and echoes blend,
I hold you close, dear Zoran, my brother, my lost friend.
And as the music lingers, in the twilight's gentle glow,
I'll carry you within me, wherever I may go.

A Daughter's Blessing

In the stillness of night, when the stars softly gleam,
You entered my life, a beautiful dream.
With hair like the midnight, so silky and bright,
You wrapped me in wonder, you filled me with light.

Those beautiful eyes, oh, how they captivate,
Windows to a soul that radiates fate.
Filled with love and compassion, a heart pure and true,
A spirit so gentle, the world's gift to you.

You've taught me the meaning of love without bounds,
In your laughter, I've found the sweetest of sounds.
With every small gesture, you've shown me the way,
To embrace every heartbeat, to cherish each day.

In your tiny hands, you hold the power to mend,
A heart so expansive, my truest best friend.
You've helped me grow stronger, like roots in the ground,
In your presence, my darling, I've finally found.

You're better than I was, in ways I can't measure,
A light in the darkness, my heart's greatest treasure.
With each passing moment, you blossom and soar,
A tapestry woven with love at its core.

As you stretch your wings, and reach for the skies,
I watch with such pride, through tear-filled eyes.
For you are my miracle, my joy, my delight,
An angel on earth, my heart's purest light.

The more that you grow, the more I can see,
The beauty within you, the wonder you'll be.
With every new challenge, you rise and you shine,
A beacon of hope, a spirit divine.

So here's to my daughter, my heart's greatest song,
In a world that can falter, you'll always be strong.
With your beautiful spirit, you'll conquer the night,
For you are my blessing, my daughter, my light.

And though time may take you, as it surely will do,
Know that in my heart, I'll always love you.
For you are my angel, my pride, my sweet star,
In this journey of life, you've shown me who we are.

A Mother's Lament

In the stillness of night, when the world fades away,
I'm haunted by echoes of things I can't say.
Each word that I spoke, a stone in your heart,
A reminder of moments that tore us apart.

Oh, my precious daughter, how I long for your grace,
But the shadows of guilt leave a mark on my face.
I battled my demons, too proud to confess,
And in my own struggle, I caused you distress.

I'm sorry for times when my anger took flight,
For the words that I hurled in the heat of the night.
It was never a lack of the love that I bear,
But the love for myself that I couldn't declare.

Each day that I'm distant, each moment I grieve,
Is a reminder of all that I failed to achieve.
I regret every silence, each tear that you cried,
The days spent apart, the love that I denied.

I wish I could turn back the hands of the clock,
To hold you, to cherish, to be your strong rock.
But the weight of my choices, the burden I bear,
Is a heavy reminder of how much I care.

I miss you, my darling, more than words can express,
In this hell of regret, I'm longing for rest.
For the unhealed parts of me that you've had to endure,
I'm sorry, my love, I'm desperate for cure.

If I could rewrite the chapters of pain,
I'd fill them with laughter, let love be the gain.
But all that I have are these words from my soul,
A plea for forgiveness, to make my heart whole.

So here I stand, broken, with love in my chest,
Hoping one day you'll find peace and rest.
For you are my treasure, my light, my sweet girl,
And I'll fight through my demons to give you this world.

With each step I take, I'll carry your name,
And strive to be better, to break free from the shame.
For you are my heart, my reason to mend,
And I'll love you forever, my daughter, my friend.

The Tapestry of Trials

In the quiet shadows where I once lay,
A soul fractured, lost, in disarray,
I'm slowly learning who I truly am,
A unique spark, a flickering flame.

With every wound, a lesson learned,
Through the fires of hell, my spirit burned,
Each trial a demon, each tear a thread,
Weaving a tapestry of the life I've led.

Rock bottom, a myth, a mere starting line,
For deeper chasms await, where the sun won't shine,
Yet here I stand, a warrior reborn,
From ashes of sorrow, a new self is worn.

I've danced with despair, I've wrestled with fate,
Thought I'd be swallowed, thought it was too late,
But through the darkness, a flicker of light,
A whisper of hope, igniting the night.

Thank you, dear demons, for shaping my core,
For teaching me strength, for opening doors,
To those who stood by, unwavering, true,
Your love was the anchor that pulled me on through.

I'm different, I know it, I wear it with pride,
In a world of the ordinary, I choose to abide,
In laughter and tears, I'll paint my own way,
For this life is a canvas, and I'm here to stay.

No "what ifs" will haunt me, no shadows of dread,
When my story is told, I'll smile instead,
For I've lived every moment, embraced every scar,
And I'll leave this world knowing just who we are.

To help those in darkness, to light up the night,
To share in their burdens, to guide them to light,
If my story inspires just one weary heart,
Then my journey is worthy, my purpose, my art.

So here's to the battles, the scars that remain,
To the beauty in struggle, the joy in the pain,
For I am a phoenix, rising anew,
And in every heartbeat, I'll carry you too.

Let the world see my journey, let the tears freely flow,
For in every drop lies the strength to grow,
And when the end comes, as it surely will,
I'll embrace it with love, with a heart that is still.

For I've learned who I am, and I'm proud of the fight,
In the tapestry of trials, I've found my own light.

When Love Transforms: A Journey of Hearts

In the bloom of youth, where laughter sings,
Two hearts entwined, like the dance of spring,
She, just eighteen, with dreams in her eyes,
He, a bright spark beneath the wide skies.

With whispers of love, they painted their days,
In the warmth of the sun, in the soft, golden rays,
A spark ignited, a fire so bright,
In the hush of the night, everything felt right.

Then came the news, a twist in their tale,
A tiny heartbeat, a love without fail,
At nineteen, she cradled her world in her hands,
A daughter, a miracle, their future, their plans.

With vows exchanged, just before she arrived,
They promised forever, their hearts intertwined,
In the chaos of diapers and lullabies sung,
They built a small kingdom, where love was still young.

But time, like a river, flows swift and unkind,
And the dreams they had woven began to unwind,
Through laughter and tears, they weathered the storm,
Yet sometimes the love that was once so warm,

Became a soft echo, a whisper of what,
Had once been a fire, now flickering, caught,
In the shadows of silence, where once there was song,
They found in each other, where they both belonged.

Twelve years of memories, both bitter and sweet,
Two souls on a journey, now finding their feet,
Sometimes love falters, and sometimes it bends,
Yet in the soft twilight, they found they were friends.

With hearts still connected, though paths drift apart,
They learned to embrace the new roles in their hearts,
For sometimes the love that once burned so bright,
Can transform into friendship, a different light.

So here's to the journey, the laughter, the tears,
To the moments that shaped them through all of the years,
For love may evolve, but it never quite dies,
In the heart of a family, where true love lies.

To the Heart That Bore Us

In the quiet of the night, when shadows softly creep,
I think of all the sacrifices, the promises you keep.
With weary hands and tired eyes, you faced the world alone,
Yet in your hearts, a fire burned, a love that's deeply sown.

Through storms that raged and trials faced, you stood, unyielding, strong,
With every tear and every prayer, you taught us to belong.
You wore your burdens like a cloak, so we could dance in light,
You gave us dreams to chase and hold, you turned our dark to bright.

Fourteen hours, day by day, you toiled without a sigh,
Each moment spent, each drop of sweat, a testament to why.
You built a future from your hopes, a tapestry of grace,
With every stitch, you wove your love, a warm and safe embrace.

I see the lines upon your face, the stories they could tell,
Of nights you spent in worry, of battles fought so well.
You gave us laughter, joy, and peace, a sanctuary true,
In every hug, in every word, we felt your love break through.

So here I stand, with grateful heart, beneath the stars above,
A child forever in your debt, for all your endless love.
For every sacrifice you made, for every dream you chased,
I thank you, dear, for all you've done, for every moment graced.

You taught us strength, you taught us hope, you showed us how to care,
In every struggle, every fight, you whispered, "We are there."
And as I walk this path of life, I carry you with me,
For in my heart, your love remains, a boundless legacy.

So let the world know of your grace, let every heart take flight,
For you are the stars that guide my way, my compass in the night.
To you, my dear, I owe it all, my future, bright and free,
Thank you, Mum and Dad, for being everything to me.

Forever 22

In the quiet of the night, I hear your laughter,
A ghostly echo, a sweet disaster.
We didn't talk as much, but you were always there,
In the heart of Darwin, in the cool night air.

The world felt safe, wrapped in your light,
Good, happy, loving – everything felt right.
But now it's cold, harsh, a ruthless expanse,
A heartless void where shadows dance.

I feel like I died when you slipped away,
Forgotten in silence, where memories fray.
The stink of grief clings, a bitter perfume,
A reminder of joy turned to sorrow and gloom.

Brotherhood lost, a bond torn apart,
You were my mirror, my soul, my heart.
Not just a friend, but my soulmate, my guide,
In a world full of chaos, you stood by my side.

There's only one Jack Aaron Neal, it's true,
"Thank fuck for that," we'd laugh, just us two.
We'd drive to the beach, let the waves kiss our feet,
In the sand, we'd talk, where the wild hearts meet.

Unapologetic, we danced in the sun,
Two brothers, two souls, forever as one.
You taught me the meaning of love without fear,
In your eyes, I found home, in your heart, I was near.

You'd kill for me, and I'd do the same,
In a world that judged, we played our own game.
But now I'm a shell, just a whisper of me,
Trying to honour the man you used to see.

My tattoo speaks volumes, a promise, a vow,
"Sive vivi, sive mortui, fratres in aeternum erimus,"
Forever, we're brothers, in life or in death,
But how do I breathe when you've stolen my breath?

You taught me to fight, to stand and to strive,
But you left me with questions, how do I survive?
How do I live in a world without you?
When every heartbeat reminds me of what's true.

Forever 22, a life cut so short,
A flame that burned bright, now a flickering thought.
I just want my brother, my friend, my light,
To share in the laughter, to make wrongs feel right.

So I carry your spirit, your love in my chest,
In the silence, I find you, in the chaos, I rest.
Though the world feels empty, and the nights are so long,
I'll keep you alive in my heart, in my song.

For every tear shed, for every sigh,
I'll honour your memory, I'll never say goodbye.
In the depths of my sorrow, I'll find a way through,
Forever my brother, I'll always love you.

Whispers in the Shadows

In the quiet hours when the world is still,
A tempest brews within, a void to fill.
The sun may rise, but shadows creep,
In the corners of my mind, where the lost souls weep.

Each morning's light, a cruel disguise,
A mask of hope that slowly dies.
I wear a smile, a fragile thread,
While demons dance in the halls of my head.

They whisper secrets, they claw and bite,
In the depths of darkness, they steal my light.
"Unworthy," they hiss, "you'll never be free,
A prisoner of sorrow, just let it be."

I fight with fists made of trembling air,
Each breath a battle, each heartbeat a snare.
The mirror reflects a face I don't know,
A ghost of a dream, a shadow of woe.

I reach for the stars, but they slip through my hands,
Like grains of sand in forgotten lands.
The laughter of others, a distant refrain,
While I drown in the echoes of my own pain.

I scream in silence, a cry unheard,
A symphony of anguish, a broken bird.
The weight of the world, a shroud on my chest,
In the depths of despair, I long for rest.

But in the abyss, a flicker remains,
A whisper of hope amidst the chains.
For every dark night, the dawn will break,
And even the heart that's shattered can wake.

So I gather my courage, though weary and worn,
To face the demons that leave me torn.
With each step forward, I reclaim my fight,
A warrior rising from the depths of the night.

Though scars may linger, and shadows may call,
I'll stand in the light, I'll rise after the fall.
For in this battle, I'm not alone,
In the heart of the storm, I'll find my home.

And when the whispers threaten to drown my soul,
I'll remember the strength that makes me whole.
For every tear shed, a seed will be sown,
In the garden of healing, I'll finally be known.

Echoes of the Unseen

In the quiet of night, when the world holds its breath,
I wrestle with shadows, I dance with my death.
A heart once so vibrant, now tethered in chains,
Each pulse a reminder of unspoken pains.

The echoes of trauma, they whisper my name,
A haunting refrain, a relentless game.
I wear my scars like a cloak in the dark,
Each mark tells a story, each wound leaves a mark.

I walk through the daylight, a mask on my face,
But inside I'm a tempest, a fractured embrace.
The laughter of others feels distant, surreal,
As I navigate mazes of what I can't feel.

"Just let it go," they say, with eyes full of light,
But they don't see the battles I fight every night.
The memories linger, like ghosts in my mind,
A tapestry woven with threads of unkind.

I'm haunted by moments that time cannot heal,
A prisoner of memories, a heart made of steel.
The world moves around me, but I'm stuck in the past,
Each second a reminder of shadows I cast.

I crave the connection, the warmth of a smile,
Yet fear it will vanish, like dreams in a trial.
I reach for the sunlight, but it burns like a flame,
A paradox living, I'm lost in the game.

The demons are patient, they whisper and tease,
They feed on my doubts, they revel in ease.
"Unworthy, unlovable," their chorus resounds,
In the silence of night, my spirit confounds.

But in this abyss, a flicker ignites,
A spark of resilience that fights through the nights.
For every dark moment, a lesson unfolds,
In the tapestry woven, my story is told.

I gather the pieces, though shattered and worn,
To embrace the chaos, to rise from the scorn.
With each breath I take, I reclaim my own voice,
A symphony rising, a heart that can rejoice.

Though the demons may linger, and shadows may loom,
I'll dance with my darkness, I'll find my own bloom.
For in this battle, I'm learning to see,
The beauty in fragments, the strength to be me.

So here I stand, with my heart on my sleeve,
A warrior of light, in the dark I believe.
For every tear shed, a bridge I will build,
In the garden of healing, my spirit fulfilled.

A Whisper in the Abyss

Oh, weary soul, on the edge of despair,
I see you there, with your heart laid bare.
The weight of the world, a burden so deep,
In the silence of night, you've forgotten to weep.

The shadows are heavy, they cling to your skin,
A battle unending, where hope feels like sin.
You're tired of fighting, of wearing this mask,
Of searching for answers to questions unasked.

But listen, dear heart, to the whispering breeze,
It carries the stories of those who've found peace.
The echoes of laughter, the warmth of a hand,
The love that surrounds you, though hard to understand.

You stand at the precipice, the void calls your name,
But beyond this dark moment, there's light yet to claim.
The stars in the heavens, they flicker and shine,
Each one a reminder that you are divine.

You are not just a shadow, a whisper of pain,
You're a tapestry woven with joy and with rain.
The storms may be fierce, but they shape who you are,
A warrior of light, a flicker, a star.

Think of the laughter, the moments of grace,
The warmth of a hug, the love in a face.
The dreams that you carry, the songs yet unsung,
The battles you've fought, the victories won.

In the depths of your sorrow, there's strength to be found,
A flicker of hope in the silence profound.
For every dark night, there's a dawn that will break,
A promise of healing, a chance to awake.

So take a deep breath, let the tears freely flow,
For grief is a river, and it's okay to know.
You're not alone in this fight that you face,
There's a world full of love, a warm, safe embrace.

Hold on, dear soul, to the flicker inside,
The spark that ignites when the darkness collides.
You are worthy of life, of laughter, of light,
A beacon of hope in the depths of the night.

So step back from the edge, let the shadows recede,
For there's beauty in living, in planting a seed.
The journey is long, but each step is a gift,
And in the heart's struggle, your spirit will lift.

You are more than the pain, more than the scars,
You're a story unfolding, a dance with the stars.
So stay, dear heart, let the dawn find your face,
For life is a journey, a beautiful grace.

Resurrection of Shadows

In the silence of a mind, where darkness reigns,
I stood at the edge, where hope wanes,
A whisper of despair, a scream in the night,
I chose to surrender, to extinguish the light.

A body adrift, a vessel unmoored,
I lost all control, my spirit ignored,
The weight of existence, too heavy to bear,
In that fleeting moment, I chose to despair.

"I'm done," said my heart, in a voice cold and clear,
"Let the silence embrace me, let go of the fear."
With a final heartbeat, I slipped from the fray,
Into the abyss, where shadows hold sway.

But life, in its mercy, had other designs,
A friend in the darkness, where fate intertwines,
With courage ignited, she stole from the hands
Of the doctors who waited, with their sterile commands.

The first jolt of thunder, a spark in the night,
But the darkness held tight, and I slipped from their sight,
Yet she would not falter, she fought through the pain,
With a second defiance, she called me again.

Zapped back to existence, on a gurney I lay,
A ghost in the limelight, where shadows betray,
I opened my eyes to the world I had fled,
But the echoes of silence still danced in my head.

What is it to live when you've tasted the end?
To walk through the ashes, to mend and to bend,
Each breath a reminder of battles once fought,
Of the moments I craved, yet the solace I sought.

I am a survivor, a soul torn apart,
With scars that are hidden, yet etched in my heart,
For every heartbeat that thrums in my chest,
Is a testament whispered, a life readdressed.

So here I stand, in the light and the dark,
A flicker of hope, a resilient spark,
For those who are lost, who wander alone,
Know that in shadows, you're never on your own.

In the depths of despair, when the mind feels like stone,
Remember the fight, the love that's been shown,
For life is a canvas, painted with pain,
And from the ashes, we rise once again.

Welcome to My Truth

Welcome to the life of a transgender male,
Where the world's harsh whispers drown out the serene.
Born into a body that felt like a cage,
A heart full of dreams, but trapped in a rage.

I didn't choose this path, this struggle, this fight,
To be ridiculed, abused, cast into the night.
To walk through the halls with my head held low,
While the laughter and judgment cut deeper than snow.

I was born in the wrong skin, a truth hard to bear,
Each day a battle, each breath a prayer.
To transition, to rise, to claim what is mine,
Is the hardest journey, a steep, jagged climb.

All I want is for the outside to match what's within,
To shed all the layers of sorrow and sin.
To be seen as I am, not judged by my form,
To find in acceptance a place that is warm.

But the world can be cruel, with its sharp, biting words,
Like arrows they pierce, like the song of the birds.
I wear tough skin, but the wounds still remain,
Each taunt, each rejection, a shadow of pain.

Yet in this darkness, a flicker of light,
A spark of resilience ignites in the night.
For every harsh word, there's a voice that will rise,
A chorus of love that shatters the lies.

I stand here, unapologetic and bold,
A story of courage, a heart made of gold.
I am more than the body that others can see,
I am the spirit, the fire, the essence of me.

So welcome to my truth, my journey, my fight,
In a world that may judge, I will shine ever bright.
For every tear shed, there's a lesson to learn,
In the ashes of sorrow, a phoenix will burn.

I am not just a label, a name, or a face,
I am a tapestry woven with strength and with grace.
So hear me, believe me, let love be the guide,
In the heart of a man, a warrior resides.

A Dreamer's Journey

In a village where the sun kissed the earth,
A child was born, full of laughter and mirth.
With eyes like the sky, so wide and so bright,
He dreamed of the stars, of soaring in flight.

"Someday," he whispered, "I'll help those in need,
With kindness and courage, I'll plant every seed.
I'll mend broken hearts, I'll heal every pain,
I'll bring back the joy, like a soft summer rain."

But shadows crept in, as darkness will do,
When the drums of war thundered, and innocence flew.
At six years of age, he was thrust into hell,
Where the echoes of anguish rang loud like a bell.

The laughter was silenced, the colours turned grey,
As the world he once knew was ripped far away.
He watched as the flames consumed all that he loved,
And the angels of mercy were nowhere above.

With each passing moment, the innocence bled,
As he clutched to his dreams, while the world filled with dread.
He saw mothers weeping, their children now lost,
And he felt the weight of a terrible cost.

Yet deep in his heart, a flicker remained,
A whisper of hope, though his spirit was strained.
"I'll rise from the ashes, I'll carry the light,
I'll be the brave beacon that shines through the night."

Years turned to decades, the scars never healed,
But the fire within him, it never concealed.
He wandered through shadows, through sorrow and strife,
With a heart full of purpose, he sought out a life.

He learned from the pain, from the tears that he shed,
That to help others rise, he must first face the dread.
He gathered the broken, the lost and the weak,
With a voice like a river, he taught them to speak.

"Together we'll stand, through the storms and the rain,
We'll build up our dreams, we'll embrace all the pain.
For in every heartache, there's a lesson to find,
In the depths of our suffering, we'll leave no one behind."

And though he was weary, with burdens to bear,
He walked with the wounded, he showed them he cared.
For the child who once dreamed, now a man forged in fire,
Had become the embodiment of hope and desire.

So remember his journey, the trials he faced,
The dreams of a child, in a world so displaced.
For in every tear shed, in every heart's ache,
Lies the strength of a spirit that no war can break.

And as the sun sets on the horizon so wide,
Know that love is the journey, and hope is the guide.
For the man who once dreamed, now stands tall and free,
A testament to courage, a soul's legacy.

Eight Years of Becoming

Today marks the day, eight years in the making,
A journey of truth, a heart slowly waking.
In shadows I wandered, in silence I cried,
A soul trapped in anguish, a spirit denied.

To those who believe that we choose this path,
Who think we embrace the scorn and the wrath,
Know this: we don't choose the laughter, the pain,
The whispers of "freak" that echo like rain.

We don't choose to be disowned, cast aside,
To wear the weight of a world that derides.
We don't choose the darkness, the threats, or the fear,
The voices that tell us our lives aren't sincere.

But here I stand, a testament true,
Eight years of courage, of breaking right through.
My heart, once a battlefield, now beats with pride,
For I am the person I've longed to confide.

My psychologist sees what the world often misses,
In a sea of confusion, she offers her kisses –
Of validation, of truth, of a life that's my own,
In a world that can shatter, I've finally grown.

It's been hell, yes, but I chose to survive,
To be my true self, to feel truly alive.
For the first time, I love every part of my days,
In laughter and friendship, in love's warm embrace.

With my best friend beside me, we rise and we fall,
He lifts me up gently, he answers my call.
Through the struggles and stumbles, we dance in the light,
In a world that can darken, we shine ever bright.

And my daughter, oh sweet one, you deserve my best,
A mother who's genuine, who's passed every test.
I'm here, I'm alive, I'm the love that you need,
In this garden of life, I've planted my seed.

So here's to the journey, the battles we've fought,
To the love that we've nurtured, the lessons we've taught.
Eight years of becoming, of shedding the skin,
Of embracing the truth, of letting love in.

Let the tears fall like rain, let the hearts break and mend,
For in every struggle, we find strength to transcend.
This is who I am, and I stand here today,
A beacon of hope in a world gone astray.

In Shadows Deep

In the silence of the night, I hear them call,
Whispers of demons, shadows that crawl,
They dance in the corners of my weary mind,
A symphony of sorrow, a fate unkind.

Each day a battle, each breath a fight,
Chained to the darkness, I long for the light.
The drug, my solace, my cruel, bitter friend,
Promises of peace, but they never quite mend.

I stood on the edge, where the shadows conspire,
A heart full of anguish, a soul lost in fire.
Thoughts like a tempest, a storm in my chest,
In the depths of despair, I longed for rest.

But in that bleak moment, a flicker appeared,
A glimmer of hope, though I trembled with fear.
Rosalie House beckoned, a beacon so bright,
A sanctuary waiting to guide me to light.

With open arms, they welcomed my pain,
Taught me to dance in the sun and the rain.
In circles of healing, I found my own voice,
In the warmth of their kindness, I made a new choice.

They showed me the beauty in scars that I bear,
That healing is messy, but love is laid bare.
Each story a thread in the tapestry spun,
Together we rise, together we run.

I learned to embrace the shadows I fought,
To face every demon, to cherish each thought.
With tools in my pocket and strength in my heart,
I'm crafting a future, a brand new start.

No longer a prisoner, I'm learning to soar,
With every small victory, I'm hungry for more.
The road may be winding, but I'm not alone,
In the arms of recovery, I've finally grown.

So here's to the journey, the battles I've won,
To the light that now shines, to the warmth of the sun.
With Rosalie House guiding, I'm learning to be,
The best version of me, finally free.

Whispers in the Dark

In the quiet hours when shadows creep,
A tempest stirs where silence weeps,
A heart encased in trembling chains,
Fights battles fought in unseen plains.

Each breath a war, each thought a knife,
A dance with demons, a struggle for life,
They whisper secrets, they claw and bite,
In the corners of my mind, they ignite the night.

"Not good enough," they hiss and sneer,
"Why even try? Just disappear."
A mirror reflects a fractured soul,
A jigsaw puzzle with pieces stole.

I wear a mask, a painted smile,
But inside I'm lost, a thousand miles,
The world spins on, oblivious, bright,
While I'm trapped in a cage, devoid of light.

I reach for hope, but it slips away,
Like grains of sand at the end of the day,
I scream for help, but the echoes fade,
In a labyrinth of fears, I'm forever betrayed.

The clock ticks on, relentless, cruel,
Time is a thief, a merciless fool,
It steals my laughter, my joy, my peace,
In the grip of this monster, I beg for release.

Yet in the darkness, a flicker remains,
A whisper of strength that softly sustains,
For every tear that falls like rain,
Is a testament to the courage in pain.

So I'll rise again, though battered and worn,
With scars as my armour, a heart reborn,
For in this battle, though weary and frail,
I'll find my voice, I'll learn to prevail.

And if you see me, know I'm not weak,
I'm a warrior forged in the silence I seek,
With every heartbeat, I'll fight and I'll stand,
For the light in my soul is a flickering brand.

So let the tears flow, let the heart break,
For in every fracture, new strength I'll make,
And though anxiety may shadow my days,
I'll dance with my demons, in my own brave ways.

Eclipsed by You

In the hush of dawn, when the world is still,
I find my heart racing, a wild, tender thrill,
For there in the light, like a dream come alive,
Is the woman who makes my very soul thrive.

Her laughter, a melody, sweet as the breeze,
It dances through shadows, puts my heart at ease,
With every glance, she ignites a fire,
A blaze of devotion, a burning desire.

Her eyes, twin galaxies, deep and profound,
In their shimmering depths, my forever is found,
Each moment with her, a treasure I keep,
A promise of love that runs oceans so deep.

When she walks in the room, the air shifts and sways,
Time holds its breath, and the sunlight obeys,
Every heartbeat echoes, a symphony played,
In the presence of magic, my worries all fade.

I've wandered through storms, I've battled the night,
But she is my compass, my guiding light,
With her hand in mine, I feel I can soar,
For she is my home, my heart's open door.

Yet, in the quiet, a whisper of fear,
What if this love, so precious, disappears?
What if the stars that we've woven so tight,
Flicker and fade in the depths of the night?

But then she turns, and the world falls away,
Her smile, a sunrise that brightens my day,
In her gaze, I see all the dreams I once lost,
A love that's unyielding, no matter the cost.

So here I stand, with my heart on my sleeve,
In the tapestry of life, she's the thread I believe,
For every heartbeat, every breath that I take,
Is a testament to love, a vow I won't break.

And if the heavens should tremble and shake,
If the ground beneath us should shatter and break,
I'll hold her close, through the chaos and strife,
For she is my heartbeat, my reason for life.

So let the world witness this love that we share,
A bond that's unbreakable, a truth that we bear,
For in her embrace, I've found my true home,
In the depths of her soul, I'll never roam alone.

With every heartbeat, I'll cherish her name,
For she is my fire, my wild, sacred flame,
And as long as I breathe, I'll love her anew,
For I am forever, madly, deeply in love with you.

Shattered Reflections

In the quiet of night, where shadows entwine,
I found her, a spark, a love so divine,
With laughter like music, she danced through my transgender soul,
A radiant light that made my heart whole.

She whispered of dreams, of passions untold,
Of exploring the depths, of being bold,
And in her embrace, I felt something new,
A warmth that ignited, a fire so true.

But the world spun around us, a tempest of change,
As she sought her own path, a journey so strange,
With a heart full of courage, she ventured to find,
A piece of herself, a love undefined.

He stood there beside her, a figure so brave,
A cis male soul, with a heart that could save,
And I watched from the shadows, my heart in a vice,
As she tasted the freedom, the thrill of the spice.

In that moment, I felt a fracture, a tear,
A longing so deep, it was hard to bear,
For she was my muse, my reason to grow,
Yet I stood on the sidelines, a heart full of woe.

She laughed and she loved, and I felt the sting,
Of knowing I'd given her the chance to take wing,
But in her bright eyes, I saw something shift,
A glimmer of doubt, a rift in the gift.

And as days turned to nights, I felt her pull away,
The warmth of her laughter began to decay,
I wanted to change, to be all that she needs,
To heal all my wounds, to plant love's seeds.

But the more that I tried, the more I could see,
That I was not enough, not the man she'd need me to be,
"You are not man enough for me," she said with a sigh,
And in that moment, my heart learned to die.

The words cut like daggers, a truth I could feel,
A shattering echo, a wound that won't heal,
For she was my everything, my light in the dark,
And now I was left with a soul torn apart.

I wanted to grow, to be better, to stand,
But love's cruelest lesson was slipping like sand,
She sought something deeper, a love I could not give,
And in her sweet freedom, I learned how to live.

Yet here in the silence, I'm lost in the pain,
A heart once so vibrant, now drenched in the rain,
For she was the one, the spark in my night,
And now I'm just shadows, devoid of her light.

So I'll carry this heartache, this love that won't fade,
A bittersweet memory, a debt that I've paid,
For she taught me to feel, to dream, and to grow,
But in the end, it's a love I must let go.

And though she has left me, I'll cherish the flame,
Of a love that was real, though it ended in shame,
For in her embrace, I found pieces of me,
And though she's not mine, she set my heart free.

Whispers in the Wind

In the quiet corners of a crowded room,
Thoughts scatter like leaves in a tempest's bloom,
A symphony of chaos, a cacophony of sound,
Where focus is a treasure, yet never to be found.

A flicker of a moment, a spark in the dark,
Ideas dance like fireflies, igniting a hopeful spark,
But just as they gather, like stars in the night,
They vanish like shadows, swallowed by fright.

The world spins in colours, too vivid, too bright,
Each whisper a thunder, each glance a new fight,
A thousand voices echo, each one a demand,
Yet the heart yearns for silence, a gentle, guiding hand.

In the mirror, a stranger, with eyes full of dreams,
But the mirror reflects only fragments and seams,
A puzzle unending, with pieces misplaced,
A heart full of longing, yet time's cruel embrace.

"Just focus," they say, as if it's a choice,
But the mind is a river, with no single voice,
It flows in all directions, a wild, restless stream,
Where hopes drift like paper boats, lost in a dream.

The weight of the world, a burden to bear,
Invisible chains that bind with despair,
While laughter surrounds, like a cruel masquerade,
The heart aches in silence, in shadows it's laid.

And in the stillness, when the night draws near,
The thoughts become monsters, feeding on fear,
They whisper of failure, of battles not won,
Of dreams that have faded, of light that's undone.

Yet within this tempest, a flicker remains,
A spark of resilience, a heart that sustains,
For in the chaos, a beauty can bloom,
A wildflower rising, defying the gloom.

So here's to the dreamers, the lost and the found,
To the hearts that keep beating, though battered and bound,
In the depths of the struggle, a truth we must see,
That even in chaos, we're beautifully free.

Let the tears fall like rain, let the heartache be known,
For in every storm, we're never alone,
Together we rise, through the shadows we tread,
With love as our compass, and hope as our thread.

Silent Symphony

In a world that spins with colours so bright,
Where laughter erupts like stars in the night,
There's a heart that beats softly, a rhythm unheard,
A symphony playing, yet no one's observed.

Eyes wide with wonder, yet clouded with fear,
A mind like a maze, where the echoes are clear,
Thoughts tumble like marbles, scattered and lost,
Each step a tightrope, each word a great cost.

In the bustling of voices, a tempest of sound,
The whispers of chaos, where solace is drowned,
A smile painted on, but the heart wears a frown,
In the silence of struggle, the world feels like a crown.

"Why can't you just join us?" they ask with a sigh,
As if bridges were simple, as if wings could just fly,
But the path is a puzzle, with pieces askew,
A dance in the shadows, where the light feels so few.

The touch of a hand, a jolt of surprise,
A world full of textures, where comfort can die,
The laughter of children, a melody sweet,
Yet the heart feels the weight of each heartbeat.

In the depths of the night, when the stars seem to fade,
Thoughts spiral like galaxies, a cosmic cascade,
The mind is a fortress, with walls built so high,
Where dreams whisper softly, but often just sigh.

And in the stillness, when the world drifts away,
The heart aches for connection, for words left to say,
For the beauty of friendship, the warmth of a glance,
Yet the fear of rejection can silence the dance.

But within this tempest, a light starts to glow,
A spark of resilience, a strength we can show,
For in every heartbeat, in every soft tear,
There's a story of courage, a voice that is clear.

So here's to the dreamers, the quiet, the bold,
To the hearts that keep shining, though weary and cold,
In the tapestry woven with threads of our pain,
We find threads of beauty, like flowers in rain.

Let the tears fall like rivers, let the heartache be known,
For in every struggle, we're never alone,
Together we rise, through the shadows we tread,
With love as our anchor, and hope as our thread.

The Solitary Path

In the quiet of shadows, where whispers reside,
A lone figure wanders, with nowhere to hide.
A heart wrapped in armour, a soul forged in steel,
The world sees the strength, but knows not how I feel.

I walk through the crowd, yet I'm lost in the throng,
A melody muted, a forgotten song.
With eyes that observe, but lips that stay sealed,
In the battle of silence, my wounds remain healed.

They call me a wanderer, a ghost in the night,
A sigma, they say, with a heart full of fight.
But beneath the bravado, the calm and the cool,
Lies a tempest of thoughts, a heart that's a fool.

For every choice made, there's a price to be paid,
In the freedom I cherish, a loneliness laid.
I've danced with the shadows, embraced the unknown,
Yet the weight of the silence can chill to the bone.

I've watched as they gather, in circles of light,
While I stand on the edges, a star out of sight.
The laughter, the banter, the bonds that they weave,
In the tapestry of life, I'm the thread that won't leave.

I've tasted the freedom, the thrill of the chase,
But the emptiness lingers, a haunting embrace.
For every adventure, there's a longing for home,
In the vastness of choices, I still feel alone.

The world sees the strength, the independence I wear,
But they don't see the battles, the weight of despair.
For in every triumph, there's a shadow that looms,
A reminder that silence can echo in rooms.

I've built my own fortress, a castle of dreams,
Yet the walls that protect me can stifle my screams.
In the stillness of night, when the stars start to fade,
I question the choices, the paths that I've made.

Am I strong or just weary, a king without kin?
A wanderer searching for where to begin.
In the depths of my heart, there's a flicker of light,
A hope that one day, I'll find my own fight.

So here's to the dreamers, the lone and the brave,
To the souls who keep searching, who long to be saved.
In the silence we carry, in the battles we face,
May we find our own solace, our own sacred space.

For in every heartbeat, in the tears that we shed,
There's a story of courage, a life that we've led.
And though we may wander, through shadows and pain,
We'll rise from the ashes, and dance in the rain.

Echoes of a Dreamer

In the cradle of dawn, where the sun first breaks,
A child with bright eyes, a heart that awakes,
He danced with the stars, whispered secrets to trees,
With dreams like wildflowers, swaying in the breeze.

"Look at him," they'd say, "so full of delight,
But don't get too close; he's not quite right."
With laughter like music, he'd spin in the light,
Yet shadows would gather, dimming his sight.

"Dumb," they would call him, "a freak, just a fool,"
Each word like a stone, each taunt a cruel tool,
He learned to wear silence, a mask made of shame,
As hope turned to whispers, and dreams lost their name.

He wanted to soar, to paint the vast skies,
But the weight of their words made him question the rise,
"Who am I to dream? What right do I own?
When the world sees a failure, a heart made of stone?"

So he buried his visions, deep down in the dark,
While the flicker of passion faded, a spark,
He walked through the years, a ghost in the crowd,
With a smile on his face, but his heart screaming loud.

Each person he met, a dagger disguised,
With promises sweet, but intentions unwise,
They'd use him, then leave, like shadows at dusk,
And he'd gather the pieces, a heart turned to rust.

"Trust me," they'd whisper, "you're safe here with me."
But the chains of his past held him down, made him flee,
He'd give all he had, just to feel like he's whole,
Yet the emptiness echoed, a void in his soul.

He watched as the years slipped like sand through his hands,
While the dreams that once danced turned to dust in the lands,
"Maybe I'm nothing," he'd murmur in pain,
"Just a flicker of hope, lost in the rain."

But deep in the silence, a voice softly cried,
"Remember the child who once soared with the tide?
He's still there, my dear, beneath layers of fear,
Waiting for courage to break through the veneer."

So he stood at the edge, where the shadows collide,
With a heart full of longing, and tears he can't hide,
For the dreams that he buried, the hopes that he lost,
Are the treasures of life, no matter the cost.

And though the world's cruel, and the journey is long,
He'll rise from the ashes, reclaiming his song,
For the child with the hope, the dreams in his eyes,
Is still there, still fighting, beneath the dark skies.

So let the tears flow, let the heartache be known,
For in every lost dream, a seed has been sown,
And though he may stumble, he'll learn to believe,
That the worth of a dreamer is the love that they weave.

From Shadows to Light: A Journey of Truth

In shadows deep, where silence dwells,
A boy once hid, with untold spells,
A heart encased in a fragile shell,
In a world that whispered, "You're not well."

He wore a mask, a heavy guise,
With every smile, he stifled cries,
In mirrors cracked, he sought his face,
But found instead a hollow space.

The demons danced in the dark of night,
With every breath, they stole his light,
They whispered lies, they fed his fears,
A symphony of uncried tears.

Innocence shattered, a violent storm,
A body violated, a spirit torn,
In the grip of shadows, he fought to breathe,
A haunting echo, a heart that grieves.

Each scar a story, each bruise a tale,
Of battles waged where hope seemed frail,
Yet in the depths of anguish, he sought,
A flicker of truth, a lesson taught.

He learned to rise from the ashes of pain,
To reclaim his name, to dance in the rain,
With every step, he shed the past,
A warrior forged, resilient and vast.

But still the nights would claw and bite,
The memories lingered, a ghostly fright,
Yet in the darkness, he found a spark,
A flicker of courage to light the dark.

He stood before the world, unmasked, unbowed,
A testament to the lost and the proud,
With every heartbeat, he claimed his right,
To love, to live, to shine his light.

So here's to the boy who fought through the night,
Who turned his pain into a beacon bright,
May his story echo, may his truth be known,
For in every struggle, we're never alone.

Let tears fall freely, let hearts intertwine,
For healing begins when we dare to define,
The strength in our stories, the power in pain,
In the tapestry of life, we rise once again.

Whispers of Innocence

In a world where laughter danced on sunlit streams,
Two children played, weaving dreams in golden beams.
With hands entwined, they chased the skies so blue,
Unaware of the shadows that silently grew.

But one fateful day, the sky turned to ash,
The laughter was silenced, the innocence crashed.
A thunderous roar, a shattering sound,
The ground trembled fiercely, the lost innocence drowned.

"Run!" cried the voices, but where could they flee?
Innocence shattered, like glass by the sea.
With eyes wide in terror, she clutched her friend tight,
As darkness descended, swallowing light.

The air filled with chaos, the cries of despair,
A symphony of horror, a nightmare laid bare.
Her heart raced like thunder, her breath caught in fear,
As she watched her best friend, the one she held dear.

A flash of bright fire, a scream torn apart,
The world turned to silence, a knife to the heart.
"Please, don't let go!" she whispered in vain,
But the echoes of laughter were lost in the pain.

The ground soaked in sorrow, the sky wept in grey,
As innocence crumbled, and hope slipped away.
"Why?" she cried softly, "What have we done?"
In a world filled with darkness, where's the light of the sun?

The screams can still be heard, even tongues torn away,
In the silence of night, where the shadows hold sway.
A child's heart now heavy, a burden to bear,
With memories of laughter, now lost in despair.

She carries the weight of a world gone astray,
A witness to horror, where children can't play.
In dreams, she still sees her friend's gentle face,
A ghost in the twilight, a lost, sacred place.

So let us remember, as we turn from the light,
The children who suffer, who tremble in fright.
For in every lost laugh, in every cruel scar,
Lies the echo of innocence, forever ajar.

In the depths of our hearts, let compassion ignite,
To shield every child from the horrors of night.
For peace is a promise, a dream we must weave,
So no child will witness the horrors we grieve.

Unveiling the Mirror

In the shadows where silence weeps,
A boy hides, his heart in chains,
Wrapped in whispers, stitched with fears,
A tapestry of unspoken pains.

He walks a path of fractured light,
A ghost in a world that feels so wrong,
Each breath a battle, each smile a mask,
In a symphony where he doesn't belong.

"I am not transitioning to kill her,"
He whispers to the night, his voice a sigh,
"I love her, I know her, she is my past,
But I am the dream that dares to fly."

His childhood echoes in the hollow halls,
A laughter lost, a shadow cast,
Yet in the depths of his aching soul,
A flicker ignites, a fire amassed.

"I need to express him, to let him breathe,
To shatter the glass that confines my heart,
He is my present, my future unbound,
In this dance of truth, I'll play my part."

The mirror reflects a fractured self,
A mosaic of dreams, both lost and found,
But with each tear, he gathers strength,
In the silence, a new voice resounds.

"The image I wear must match what I see,
For the soul knows no gender, no cage,
I am the same, in this body reborn,
A phoenix emerging from sorrow's stage."

With trembling hands, he lifts the veil,
Each layer peeled, a story untold,
The boy who was lost now stands in the light,
A warrior of truth, fierce and bold.

No longer a whisper, he roars with pride,
His heart a drum, a thunderous beat,
In the tapestry woven of love and pain,
He finds his rhythm, his soul's retreat.

So let the world see his radiant face,
Let them witness the beauty of change,
For in every tear that has fallen like rain,
Is the strength of a spirit, wild and strange.

"I am me," he declares, with arms open wide,
A symphony of colours, a vibrant embrace,
In the mirror, he sees not just a reflection,
But the essence of love, the power of grace.

And as the shadows begin to recede,
The boy who was lost now stands tall and free,
In the heart of the storm, he's found his way home,
For the truth of his being is simply to be.

Shattered Dreams

In the quiet dawn, he stood so tall,
A heart ablaze, he would not fall.
With dreams like stars, he reached for the sky,
A fire in his soul, a fierce battle cry.

Pride in his chest, determination his guide,
He chased the horizon, with hope as his stride.
Each step a promise, each breath a vow,
He'd conquer the mountains, he'd show them just how.

But shadows crept in, with whispers so sweet,
A serpent of solace, a venomous treat.
With a smile like poison, it lured him away,
And the dreams that once soared began to decay.

In the grip of the night, he lost his way,
The light in his eyes dimmed, faded to grey.
Meth became master, a thief in the dark,
Stealing his laughter, extinguishing spark.

He danced with despair, a waltz of the damned,
Each high a betrayal, each low a command.
A puppet of chaos, he spun in the void,
The dreams he once cherished, now shattered, destroyed.

He stood on the edge, with a heart full of scars,
A survivor of shadows, beneath the cold stars.
With each overdose, he brushed death's embrace,
Yet life held him captive, a cruel, bitter chase.

He tried to escape, with a blade to his skin,
But the battle within felt like losing again.
He whispered to darkness, "I'm ready to go,"
But the dawn always broke, with its merciless glow.

He's not afraid of dying, it's living that haunts,
The echoes of laughter, the ghosts of his wants.
In the silence of night, when the world fades away,
He wrestles with demons that refuse to obey.

Tears fall like rain, on a heart made of glass,
Each drop a reminder of the dreams that won't last.
He's a soldier of sorrow, a warrior of pain,
Fighting for freedom, but shackled in chains.

Yet in the abyss, a flicker remains,
A whisper of hope, through the sorrow and stains.
For even in darkness, a spark can ignite,
A flicker of courage, a will to fight.

So here's to the dreamer, the lost and the broken,
To the words left unspoken, the love left unbroken.
May you find your way back, through the shadows you roam,
For even in darkness, you're never alone.

In the depths of despair, let your spirit take flight,
For the dawn will come softly, after the night.
And though the road's heavy, and the journey is long,
Remember, dear heart, you are still so strong.

For Hamish,
My Heart's Whisper

In the quiet corners of my weary days,
You came, a soft shadow, in gentle, golden rays.
With eyes like twilight, deep and wise,
You see the storms that brew behind my skies.

A tiny heartbeat, a purr like a song,
In your presence, I find where I belong.
You curl in my lap, a warm, furry balm,
In your silent embrace, I discover my calm.

When the world feels heavy, and hope slips away,
You nudge at my heart, teach me how to stay.
With every soft meow, every playful chase,
You paint my life with love's tender grace.

Through nights of despair, when shadows creep near,
You nestle beside me, a promise so clear.
Your whiskers brush tears that fall like the rain,
In your gaze, I find solace, a refuge from pain.

You teach me of love, pure and unbound,
In your gentle spirit, true joy can be found.
No judgment, no fear, just a bond that we share,
In the depths of my sorrow, you show me you care.

Oh, Hamish, my dear, my heart's quiet plea,
You save me from darkness, you set my soul free.
In the tapestry woven of moments we spin,
You are my light, my moon, my sun within.

As I sit here in stillness, the tears start to flow,
For the love that you give, for the joy that you sow.
With every soft purr, every playful leap,
You fill my heart's garden, where love runs deep.

So I cherish each moment, each glance, and each sigh,
For you are my treasure, my sweet little guy.
In the laughter and warmth, in the quiet and strife,
You save my life daily, my beautiful life.

Together we wander, through sunshine and rain,
In the tapestry of love, we'll dance through the pain.
For as long as you're with me, my heart will remain,
Forever entwined, through joy and through pain.

The Weight of Their Dreams

In the quiet of dawn, when the world starts to wake,
A heart beats in silence, a soul starts to break.
With each breath a burden, each step a façade,
A puppet on strings, in a life that feels flawed.

They painted a picture, a canvas so bright,
With colours of futures, of dreams taking flight.
But the brush strokes of love turned to shadows of fear,
As the whispers of "perfect" grew louder each year.

"Be better, be stronger, achieve and succeed,"
Their voices like daggers, planting doubt like a seed.
In the mirror, a stranger, with eyes full of pain,
A reflection of dreams that feel heavy as chains.

The laughter of childhood, now echoes of shame,
As the weight of their wishes becomes my own blame.
I wear their ambitions like armour of stone,
But inside I'm a tempest, a heart all alone.

Each "I'm proud of you" feels like a knife,
Cutting deeper and deeper, erasing my life.
For what is the cost of their love, I now see,
When the price is my spirit, my essence, my me?

I dance to their rhythm, a song I don't know,
With each note a reminder of how far I'll go.
But the melody falters, the harmony fades,
As I search for my voice in the silence it made.

The demons come creeping, with whispers so sly,
"Are you enough? Will you ever comply?"
They claw at my heart, they gnaw at my soul,
In a battle for freedom, I'm losing control.

I scream in the night, but the echoes fall flat,
For the world doesn't hear me, it's too busy to chat.
"Just try a bit harder, just give it your all,"
But the harder I try, the more I feel small.

In the depths of my mind, where the shadows reside,
I'm a ghost of their dreams, with nowhere to hide.
Each tear that I shed is a story untold,
Of a heart that is weary, of a spirit grown cold.

And yet, in the darkness, a flicker ignites,
A whisper of courage, a will to take flight.
For beneath all the pressure, beneath all the pain,
Lies a spark of defiance, a hope to reclaim.

So I gather my pieces, though scattered and torn,
And I rise from the ashes, reborn from the scorn.
For I am not theirs, I am more than their dreams,
I am the storm, I am the light that redeems.

To the children still fighting, who wear the same chains,
Know that you're worthy, despite all the pains.
For the love that you seek, it must come from within,
And the journey to freedom is where you begin.

So let the tears flow, let the heartache be real,
For in the depths of your sorrow, you'll learn how to heal.
And though the road's heavy, and the journey is long,
Remember, dear heart, you are still so strong.

In the Shadow of My Heart

In the quiet corners of my mind,
Where shadows dance and whispers bind,
I wear my heart like tattered cloth,
A fragile truth, a silent oath.

They told me strength was forged in steel,
That tears were signs of wounds that heal,
"Be a man," they said, "don't show your pain,
Hide your heart, let the storm wane."

But here I stand, a trembling soul,
A vessel cracked, yet still made whole,
Each tear a testament, each sigh a song,
In the depths of sorrow, I've learned to belong.

I've battled demons, fierce and wild,
In the mirror's gaze, I see the child,
The one who felt too much, too deep,
Who wore his heart like a cloak, not a sheath.

"Too soft," they sneered, "not man enough,"
As if the heart's embrace was a sign of bluff,
But in the softness lies a strength untold,
A courage to feel, a spirit bold.

I've walked through fire, I've danced with doubt,
In the silence of night, I've screamed and shouted,
For every wound that's carved my skin,
A story of battles, a war within.

I've learned that vulnerability is not a flaw,
But a bridge to the world, a sacred law,
To open my heart, to let the light in,
To embrace the chaos, to let the love spin.

So here I stand, unashamed, unbound,
In the depths of my sorrow, my strength is found,
For every tear that falls like rain,
Is a testament to love, to joy, to pain.

I am not weak; I am not less,
I am a tapestry of tenderness,
A warrior forged in the fires of grief,
In the arms of vulnerability, I find my relief.

So let them whisper, let them scorn,
In the cradle of softness, a new heart is born,
For in the depths of my soul, I see,
That being vulnerable is the bravest me.

And when the world feels heavy and cold,
I'll wear my heart like a shield of gold,
For in the embrace of my tender fight,
I find my power, my truth, my light.

The Grave I Dig

You handed me the shovel, but I was the one
Digging my own grave the whole time,
Each thrust of earth a whisper,
Each clump of soil a silent crime.
Tossing in the parts you didn't want,
The fragments of me that once danced in the light,
Now buried beneath the weight of your indifference,
Slowly dying, pieces at a time.

It's so sad,
How a starving soul
Will devour deception
Like a delicacy,
When they think there is nothing else
To satisfy the hunter inside,
The relentless ache that gnaws,
The hollow echo of love denied.

I feasted on your promises,
Sweet morsels laced with lies,
Each bite a fleeting moment,
Each taste a bitter sigh.
You painted dreams in colours bright,
But they faded in the dark,
And I, a moth to your flame,
Burned in the shadows of your spark.

But as I dug deeper,
Searching for the love you swore was true,
I felt a flicker, a whisper,
A glimmer breaking through.
For even in this grave I've made,
Where sorrow seems to reign,
I sense the stir of something new,
A hope that blooms from pain.

The earth may hold my heartache,
But it cannot claim my soul,
For buried deep within the dark,
There lies a seed, a goal.
A promise of tomorrow,
A chance to rise again,
To shed the weight of yesterday,
And learn to love, to mend.

So here I stand,
In this grave I've made my own,
A monument to longing,
But not a place to call my home.
And as the darkness closes in,
I lift my eyes to skies above,
For even in this silent tomb,
I still believe in love.

For love, it seems,
Is a river that flows on,
A current strong and steady,
A light that won't be gone.
And as I lay beneath the weight,
Of all the dreams I couldn't save,
I know that from this quiet place,
I'll rise, I'll learn, I'll brave.

So let the past be buried,
Let the hurt become the ground,
For in the soil of my heartache,
New love will soon be found.
And as I turn to face the dawn,
With hope as my guiding star,
I'll dig not just a grave, but a garden,
Where love can grow, and heal the scars.

In Search of a Heartbeat

In the quiet corners of a restless night,
Where shadows dance with dreams of light,
I wandered through the echoes of my mind,
Chasing whispers of a love I hoped to find.

The world spun tales of lovers entwined,
Of souls ignited, of hearts aligned,
Yet in the mirror, I saw only me,
A fractured reflection, longing to be free.

I wore my heart like a tattered cloak,
Each thread a promise, each stitch a joke,
For every face that smiled, a ghost would rise,
A haunting reminder of unfulfilled ties.

I fought the demons that clawed at my chest,
The fear of forever, the ache of unrest,
With every heartbeat, I searched for the spark,
In crowded rooms, I felt so stark.

I chased the sunsets, I danced in the rain,
I climbed every mountain, I embraced every pain,
But love, it seemed, was a distant star,
A flicker of hope, yet always too far.

Then one fateful day, in the midst of despair,
A laughter broke through, a breath of fresh air,
You stood there, a beacon, a light in the haze,
With eyes that held stories, a warmth that stays.

Not a lover, but a friend, a soul laid bare,
In your presence, I found a love rare,
We shared our secrets, our fears, our dreams,
In the tapestry of life, we wove our seams.

You saw the shadows that danced in my heart,
The scars that I carried, the pieces apart,
And in your embrace, I found my release,
A bond forged in fire, a sanctuary of peace.

We laughed until tears streamed down our cheeks,
In the silence, we spoke, in the chaos, we peaked,
You held my hand through the storms and the strife,
In the depths of your friendship, I found my life.

No longer a searcher, no longer alone,
In the heart of a friend, I found my home,
For love wears many faces, and sometimes it's true,
The soulmate you seek is the one standing with you.

So here's to the journey, the battles we've fought,
To the love that we found, the lessons we've taught,
In the tapestry woven with threads of our pain,
I discovered my soulmate, and I'll never be the same.

In the quiet corners of a restless night,
I no longer wander, for you are my light,
Together we rise, together we stand,
In the heart of a friend, I found love unplanned.

Two Years in the Abyss

Two years – what weight in whispered breaths,
A fleeting echo, yet a chasm deep,
Where shadows dance and demons weave their threads,
In the silence, where the broken hearts weep.

I stood at rock bottom, a hollow shell,
In the grip of darkness, I sipped with the damned,
Each shot a promise, each laugh a farewell,
As the devil grinned, and my soul was unplanned.

I lost my compass, my guiding light,
A Queen who taught me love's unyielding grace,
Her laughter, a melody that pierced the night,
Now a haunting refrain in this desolate space.

Three friends, like stars, extinguished too soon,
Their laughter now echoes in the void of my mind,
Each memory a dagger, each smile a wound,
In the tapestry of grief, I'm forever entwined.

I was shattered, a vessel cracked wide,
When the news struck like thunder, a bolt from the blue,
My heart, a fragile bird, lost in the tide,
Yet in that moment, I found something true.

For in the depths of despair, a flicker ignites,
A spark of resilience, a whisper of hope,
Through the ashes of sorrow, I learned to take flight,
To rise from the ruins, to learn how to cope.

I miss him each day, a ghost in my chest,
Yet I feel him beside me, a warmth in the cold,
Closer than ever, in dreams he's a guest,
In the tapestry of love, our stories unfold.

So here I stand, a man forged in pain,
With scars that tell tales of battles once fought,
Each tear a testament, each loss not in vain,
For in the depths of the abyss, my soul has been sought.

Two years – what weight in whispered breaths,
A journey through hell, yet I've found my way home,
In the heart of the darkness, I've danced with my death,
And emerged from the shadows, no longer alone.

So let the world weep for the souls that we've lost,
For in every heartache, a lesson is sown,
In the tapestry of life, we bear every cost,
And from the ashes of sorrow, we rise, we have grown.

To My Beautiful Daughter

In the quiet dawn of your first breath,
A symphony of joy, a love unmeasured,
The moment you cried, the world fell away,
And in that heartbeat, my heart was tethered.

You, my light, my laughter, my grace,
With chocolate-stained hands and a mischievous smile,
You painted my life in colours so bright,
Yet I took for granted each fleeting while.

Seventeen years, a blink, a sigh,
In the tapestry of time, I wove my regrets,
Choices like shadows, haunting my days,
Yet you, my darling, are the sun that sets.

Oh, how I wish I could rewrite the past,
To hold you close, to never let go,
But the plane took me far, and the distance grew vast,
Leaving my heart in a place I can't show.

The day I departed, your tears like rain,
Each drop a reminder of love's heavy cost,
I left a piece of me, a fragment of pain,
In the echoes of laughter, in the warmth of your frost.

Now, as you stand on the brink of your dreams,
Graduation's light shining bright in your eyes,
I ache to be there, to witness your gleam,
To celebrate you, my heart's sweetest prize.

You've blossomed, my love, into a woman so rare,
With courage and kindness, a spirit so bold,
And though miles divide us, my heart is laid bare,
In every heartbeat, your story is told.

Forgive me, my darling, for moments I missed,
For the times I was lost in my own tangled fight,
But know that my love, like the stars in the mist,
Is boundless, eternal, a beacon of light.

Congratulations, my daughter, on this day of your grace,
You've conquered the trials, you've risen above,
And though I am far, in my heart you'll always have space,
For you are my treasure, my endless love.

To the moon and back, my promise remains,
In the depths of my soul, you're forever entwined,
I miss you, I love you, through heartache and pains,
You are my heart's echo, my spirit's design.

To Those Battling the Black Dog

In the stillness of dawn, when the world starts to wake,
There's a heaviness clinging, a heart that can't shake,
The sheets wrap around you like chains made of dread,
As the whispers of darkness invade your soft head.

You rise with the sun, but your spirit feels lead,
Each step feels like climbing a mountain instead,
The mirror reflects back a stranger, a ghost,
A shell of the person you once loved the most.

Long showers become sanctuaries, a refuge from pain,
Where the water can wash away tears like the rain,
But the thoughts swirl like storms, relentless and loud,
In the silence, they gather, a suffocating shroud.

You hit the gym, seeking solace in sweat,
But the demons are lurking, their grip isn't set,
You lift weights like burdens, you run from the fight,
Yet the shadows keep chasing, they haunt you at night.

Day after day, you don your brave face,
While inside you're crumbling, lost in the race,
You clock in, you smile, you play your part well,
But the truth is a prison, a personal hell.

"Just cheer up," they say, "It will all be okay,"
But they don't see the battles that rage day by day,
They don't know the struggle, the weight of the load,
The journey you travel, the dark, winding road.

To those who feel trapped in a pit of despair,
Who fight with the black dog, who feel no one cares,
Know that you're seen, in your silence, your fight,
You're warriors of shadows, you're stars in the night.

I stand with you now, in this moment of truth,
With respect for your courage, your unyielding proof,
That even when broken, you rise from the fall,
You're not alone in this; together we'll stand tall.

So here's to the fighters, the ones who endure,
To the hearts that are heavy, yet still seek the cure,
You are not just surviving; you're learning to thrive,
In the depths of the struggle, you're learning to strive.

Let the world see your scars, let them know of your fight,
For in sharing your story, you'll ignite the light,
And though the black dog may linger and grow,
You are stronger than shadows, more powerful than woe.

So take heart, dear soul, as you navigate pain,
For the sun will break through, and you'll dance in the rain,
You are not alone; we're a chorus of might,
Together we'll rise, together we'll fight.

A Tribute to Elspeth Cook

In the quiet corners of a classroom bright,
Where words took flight and dreams ignited,
You stood, Elspeth Cook, a beacon of light,
Guiding us through the realms of the written and cited.

With passion and grace, you opened our eyes,
To the beauty of language, the power of prose,
You taught us to soar, to reach for the skies,
To find our own voices, to let our hearts expose.

Each lesson a treasure, each word a new key,
Unlocking the magic that lay deep within,
You believed in my dreams when no one could see,
Encouraging the spark that would soon begin.

Through sonnets and stories, through essays and rhymes,
You nurtured my spirit, you watered the seed,
With every critique, you helped me climb,
To heights I had feared, to the places I'd need.

Now, as I pen poems, my heart full of thanks,
I carry your wisdom, your lessons, your care,
For the book that I write, in its pages, it ranks,
As a tribute to you, for the love that we share.

Elspeth Cook, your name echoes in lines,
In the rhythm of verses, in the dance of the words,
You've shaped my journey, like the finest designs,
A mentor, a guide, in a world that's absurd.

So here's to the teacher who believed in my fight,
Who saw in me potential, who sparked my desire,
With gratitude flowing, like stars in the night,
Thank you, dear Elspeth, for lighting my fire.

In the Echo of a Crowd

In a room alive with laughter,
Where voices dance like fireflies,
I stand, a shadow in the shimmer,
A ghost beneath the vibrant skies.

They smile, they reach, they care,
Yet I wear a mask, a fragile guise,
For in their warmth, I feel the chill,
A hollow heart that never lies.

I hear the music, sweet and bright,
But it's a symphony I cannot play,
Each note a reminder of my plight,
Each chord a ghost that leads astray.

I watch their joy, a distant star,
While I'm anchored in this sea of grey,
Their hands entwined, their spirits soar,
And I'm the whisper that fades away.

The demons dance within my mind,
With claws that scratch and teeth that bite,
They feast on hope, they steal the light,
In the silence, they ignite the night.

I raise a glass, I join the cheer,
But inside, I'm crumbling, lost, alone,
A castle built on shifting sand,
A heart that's turned to cold, hard stone.

They ask me how I've been, I smile,
And weave a tale of sunlit days,
But in the depths, the shadows pile,
And drown the truth in endless grey.

I long to scream, to break the chains,
To tear the mask and let them see,
The aching void, the silent pains,
The weight of all that's left of me.

But fear holds tight, a vice-like grip,
What if they turn, what if they flee?
So I swallow hard, I take a sip,
And drown the cries that long to be.

In this crowded room, I stand apart,
A lighthouse lost in fog and storm,
With every laugh, I feel the dart,
Of loneliness, a heart forlorn.

So here I linger, a silent plea,
In the echo of their joy, I drown,
For in this crowd, I cannot see,
The love that's there, the warmth around.

And as the night begins to fade,
I slip away, a fleeting ghost,
For in the light, I'm still afraid,
That I am not what they love most.

So I'll carry this ache, this heavy shroud,
A secret burden, a silent fight,
In a room alive, yet lost in the crowd,
I'll wear my loneliness, my quiet night.

And maybe one day, I'll find the words,
To break the silence, to let them in,
But for now, I'll hide, unheard,
In the echo of a crowd, where I've always been.

In the Shadow of Their Love

In the cradle of their laughter, I was born,
A child of light, yet cloaked in storm,
With dreams that danced like fireflies at dusk,
But shadows whispered, "You're not enough."

"Hormones are the cause," they said with disdain,
As if my heart was a puzzle, a riddle of pain,
"Friends pushed you into this," they claimed with a sigh,
But they don't see the truth that lives in my eye.

I wore their love like a shroud, heavy and tight,
A mask of their making, a ghost in the night,
Each word a dagger, each glance a cold chain,
Binding my spirit, drowning my name.

I fought with the demons that clawed at my soul,
In the silence of midnight, I searched for control,
With every heartbeat, a battle, a war,
To claim my own body, to open the door.

But acceptance was a garden, overgrown with their fears,
And I, a wildflower, choked by their tears,
"Why can't you see me?" I cried to the stars,
"Why can't you love me, with all of my scars?"

I longed for their arms, a sanctuary warm,
But their love felt like thunder, a tempest, a storm,
"Why can't you be normal?" their voices would sneer,
As I stood on the edge, drowning in fear.

Each day was a battle, each moment a fight,
To be seen as I am, to step into the light,
But the weight of their judgment, a mountain to climb,
Left me gasping for breath, lost in the grime.

I am not a mistake, nor a phase to outgrow,
I am the truth of my heart, the love I bestow,
Yet here in the silence, their echoes remain,
A symphony of sorrow, a chorus of pain.

So I gather my courage, I rise from the dust,
For love is a journey, and I am its trust,
Though their hearts may be closed, and their minds may be blind,
I'll carve out my path, leave their shadows behind.

In the tapestry woven with threads of my tears,
I'll find my own family, through laughter and fears,
For love is not bound by the blood that we share,
But by the souls that embrace us, the hearts that still care.

So here's to the warriors, the brave and the bold,
To those who are shattered, yet still seek the gold,
In the depths of rejection, we rise and we stand,
For we are the future, we are love's own hand.

And though they may falter, and turn from the light,
I'll carry my truth, I'll continue the fight,
For in the end, it's not them who define,
The beauty of living, the power of mine.

Shattered Whispers

I don't want your love,
If it's just a hollow shell,
A whisper in the darkness,
A fleeting, empty spell.
I stand amidst the ruins,
A mosaic of my pain,
Each shard a silent witness,
To the storms I've fought in vain.

I don't need you to complete me,
For I am whole in my despair,
A tapestry of heartache,
Woven with the threads of care.
My pieces tell a story,
Of battles lost and won,
Of demons that I've wrestled,
And the shadows that I've spun.

So if you dare to love me,
Embrace my jagged edge,
For sometimes I might cut you,
And leave you on the ledge.
My heart, it bleeds like rivers,
A torrent of unspoken fears,
Yet in this storm of sorrow,
I've learned to dry my tears.

I'm not a fragile flower,
Petals soft and sweetly pressed,
I'm the broken, growing weeds,
In the soil of my unrest.
So many tried to kill me,
With their words like poisoned darts,
But I rise from every wound,
With a fire in my heart.

They scattered glass upon the wind,
Thinking they could break my soul,
But I am forged in fire,
And I am learning to be whole.
For every cut that stings me,
Is a lesson I embrace,
In the chaos of my being,
I find my sacred space.

So love me in my darkness,
In the shadows where I dwell,
For I am more than broken,
I am a story yet to tell.
And if you choose to walk with me,
Through the shards and through the pain,
Know that in this heart of glass,
A fierce and wild love remains.

Echoes of the Abyss

In the silence of the night, when shadows stretch and creep,
A whisper calls my name, from the depths where demons sleep.
They dance upon my memories, with laughter cold and cruel,
Each echo a reminder, of the chains that make me their fool.

I wear my scars like armour, each mark a tale of woe,
A map of all my battles, in a war no one can know.
The world sees just the surface, the mask I've learned to wear,
But beneath the painted smile, lies a heart stripped bare.

I chase the fleeting solace, in the haze of smoke and glass,
A moment's sweet distraction, from the pain that's built to last.
But every high is fleeting, a cruel and bitter jest,
For when the light is fading, I'm left with all the rest.

The shame wraps 'round my spirit, like a shroud I cannot shed,
Each judgment like a dagger, each glance a thread of dread.
"Just quit," they say so easily, as if it's just a choice,
But they don't hear the whispers, of the demons in my voice.

They don't know the hunger, the gnawing, endless need,
The way it steals my laughter, and plants a bitter seed.
I'm a ghost in my own body, a stranger in my skin,
Searching for redemption, in the chaos deep within.

I've lost so many battles, to the darkness that I crave,
And every time I stumble, I feel the world's disdain.
"Why can't you just be stronger? Why can't you just be free?"
But they don't see the prison, that's built inside of me.

I'm haunted by the faces, of those I've left behind,
The friends who turned to shadows, the love I couldn't find.
Each tear that falls is heavy, a weight I cannot bear,
For every drop is laced with guilt, and the burden of despair.

Yet in this endless struggle, a flicker starts to glow,
A whisper of forgiveness, in the depths of all this woe.
I'm learning to be gentle, with the pieces of my soul,
To find the strength in weakness, and let the broken be whole.

So if you see me falter, if you see me lose my way,
Remember that I'm fighting, in the shadows where I sway.
For every step I take is courage, every breath a silent plea,
To break the chains of stigma, and finally set me free.

Let's shatter all the silence, let's speak the truth aloud,
For in the depths of darkness, we can rise and be proud.
Together we'll find healing, in the stories that we share,
For in the heart of struggle, there's a love that's always there.

Echoes of Worthlessness

It's not the darkness that consumes, but the weight of careless words,
The laughter that cuts deeper, than the sharpest of swords.
In the silence of my struggle, where shadows twist and twine,
I bear the scars of others, their indifference, my design.

Humans are allowed to falter, to stumble, trip, and fall,
Yet here I stand, a prisoner, with no chance to recall.
Each misstep is a mountain, each failure, a heavy stone,
While they walk free and easy, I'm left to face this alone.

I saved your life, a hero, yet you turned your back on me,
No gratitude, no kindness, just the void of apathy.
I gave you all my heart, but you saw it as a game,
A fleeting moment's pleasure, and I'm left with all the shame.

You had me wrapped in promises, in dreams that felt so real,
But I was just a vessel, a toy for you to feel.
I'm nothing but a shadow, a whisper in the night,
A ghost of what was once me, fading out of sight.

I'm nothing and I'm nobody, a name lost in the crowd,
A heart that beats in silence, a soul that's never loud.
I'm the echo of a heartbeat, that no one cares to hear,
A life that's filled with sorrow, a heart that's gripped by fear.

Everyone would be better, if I just slipped away,
For in this world of chaos, I'm just a price to pay.
I can't make mistakes when I'm gone, no more burdens to bear,
But the truth is, in this silence, I'm still gasping for air.

I'm drowning in the shadows, in the depths of my despair,
Each breath a heavy struggle, each moment, a silent prayer.
I long for just a whisper, a sign that I am seen,
But the world keeps on spinning, and I'm lost in what has been.

So here I stand, a specter, a testament to pain,
A story left unspoken, in the pouring, endless rain.
But if you hear my echo, if you feel my silent plea,
Know that I am still fighting, to reclaim what's left of me.

For in the heart of darkness, there's a flicker yet to find,
A spark of hope, a whisper, that I'm more than what's defined.
I'll rise from all the ashes, I'll break these chains of shame,
For even in the shadows, I can still ignite a flame.

The Battle Within

Some days I'm a tempest, a whirlwind of doubt and fear,
Lost in the chaos of my thoughts, where shadows whisper near.
I'm a mess, a beautiful wreck, a tapestry of scars,
Each thread a tale of courage, each tear a glimpse of stars.

I don't know if I'm coming, or if I'm going, lost at sea,
But I live each moment fiercely, in the rawness of just me.
No games, no masks, no pretense, what you see is what you get,
A heart laid bare, a soul exposed, in the truth, I won't forget.

I may not sugarcoat the world, or play nice to fit the mold,
But I'll speak the truth, unfiltered, with a fire that won't grow cold.
I'm a handful, they say, but I'm a handful of the best,
Passion, determination, courage, a spirit that won't rest.

Forgive me if I don't seek your permission to be free,
I won't apologise for living, for the person I must be.
I'm too fiery for the timid, too sassy for the meek,
But in my heart, I know my worth, in the strength of every peak.

I've battled demons in the night, fought the whispers of despair,
Each victory a testament, to the courage I still wear.
I've wrestled with the shadows, that tried to dim my light,
But I rise, a phoenix burning, in the depths of endless night.

I know I'm not for everyone, and that's a truth I've learned,
But to those who see my spirit, to my people, I've returned.
I'm good to those who get me, who embrace my wild embrace,
In the chaos of my being, they find beauty in the grace.

So here I stand, unyielding, with a heart that beats so loud,
A warrior forged in fire, unapologetically proud.
For every battle that I've fought, for every tear I've shed,
I've carved a path of authenticity, in the life that I have led.

So let the world keep turning, let the judgments come and go,
I'll dance in my own rhythm, in the truth that I now know.
For I am more than just a mess, I'm a symphony of soul,
A testament to living, in a world that takes its toll.

And if my fire burns too bright, if my spirit's too alive,
Know that in this fierce existence, I've learned how to survive.
I'm a handful, yes, it's true, but I'm a handful of the best,
In the battle of my heart and mind, I've found my place to rest.

Unseen Beauty

In the quiet corners of your mind,
Where shadows dance and linger,
You hold the weight of every fault,
Each flaw a jagged finger.
You wear your mistakes like heavy chains,
A cloak of doubt and shame,
But those who love you see beyond,
They know you are not to blame.

When you feel the world is ugly,
And your reflection brings you pain,
They remember the light that flickers,
The beauty that will remain.
In the depths of your despair,
When you feel so far from whole,
They gather the pieces of your heart,
And cradle your weary soul.

You may see a shattered mirror,
A thousand shards of guilt,
But they see the innocence within,
The love that you have built.
When confusion clouds your purpose,
And the path ahead seems lost,
They whisper truths to guide you,
Reminding you of the cost.

For every tear that stains your cheek,
Every moment you feel small,
They stand as pillars of your worth,
To catch you when you fall.
They know the battles you have fought,
The wars that rage inside,
And in the chaos of your heart,
They are the calm, the tide.

So when you feel unworthy,
When darkness claims your sight,
Remember those who love you,
Who see your inner light.
They hold your beauty in their hearts,
A treasure, pure and true,
And in their eyes, you are the stars,
The dawn breaking anew.

You are not defined by shadows,
Nor by the weight of your past,
For those who love you see the truth,
A love that's built to last.
They gather your scattered pieces,
And weave them into grace,
In the tapestry of your existence,
You find your rightful place.

So let the world be heavy,
Let the storms rage and roar,
For those who love you stand beside,
And they will love you more.
In every moment of your struggle,
In every doubt you face,
They remember your beauty,
And hold you in their embrace.

You are whole, you are worthy,
You are more than you can see,
For those who love you know the truth –
You are forever free.
So when the darkness whispers lies,
And you feel you've lost your way,
Remember, love is always there,
To guide you through the fray.

Awakening the Soul

In the stillness of the night, when the world is draped in dreams,
A whisper stirs within the heart, a flicker of forgotten beams.
It calls to the depths of longing, where shadows weave their thread,
A yearning for a purpose, a path where hope is fed.

With every breath, a question, a haunting echo in the dark,
"What am I, if not a wanderer, searching for a spark?"
The days stretch long and heavy, each moment a silent plea,
To break the chains of doubt and fear, to finally set the spirit free.

But the road is fraught with heartache, with echoes of the past,
Each step a dance with sorrow, each stumble a shadow cast.
The dreams once bright and vivid, now faded, worn, and torn,
Yet still, the heart keeps beating, in the silence, hope is born.

Through valleys deep with anguish, and mountains steep with pain,
The soul begins its journey, through the storm, through the rain.
With every tear that falls like rain, a seed of strength is sown,
In the soil of despair, a garden of purpose grown.

The nights are long and restless, with questions that pierce the soul,
"Am I enough? Am I worthy? Will I ever feel whole?"
But in the depths of darkness, a flicker starts to rise,
A flame ignites the spirit, a truth that never lies.

For purpose is not a destination, but a journey, raw and real,
It's found in the moments of struggle, in the wounds that time can heal.
It's in the laughter shared with strangers, in the love that breaks the mold,
In the courage to keep moving, when the heart feels tired and cold.

And as the dawn breaks softly, with colours bold and bright,
The soul begins to awaken, emerging from the night.
With every heartbeat, every breath, a symphony of grace,
The purpose once elusive, now dances in its place.

So let the tears fall freely, let the heartache wash away,
For in the depths of sorrow, the soul finds its way.
Embrace the pain, the beauty, the journey that unfolds,
For in the search for purpose, the heart becomes pure gold.

And when you stand in the sunlight, with the weight of the world behind,
You'll know you've found your purpose, a treasure intertwined.
For life is but a canvas, and you, the artist bold,
With every stroke of passion, your story will be told.

So rise, dear heart, and listen, to the whispers of your soul,
For in the quest for meaning, you will finally feel whole.
And though the path may twist and turn, with shadows lurking near,
Remember, in the search for purpose, you are the light, my dear.

In the Depths of Shadow

In the quiet corners of a restless mind,
Where whispers of the past entwine,
There lies a darkness, thick and deep,
A haunting echo, a secret to keep.

Beneath the surface, where the light dares not tread,
Lurk the demons of words left unsaid,
They dance in the shadows, they gnash and they bite,
Feeding on fears that shatter the night.

I venture forth, a trembling heart,
To face the fragments that tore me apart,
Each memory a ghost, each tear a stone,
In the labyrinth of sorrow, I walk alone.

The weight of regret, a shroud on my chest,
A symphony of anguish, a relentless quest,
I sift through the ashes of dreams turned to dust,
In the ruins of hope, I search for the trust.

Oh, the rage that simmers, the grief that consumes,
The laughter that echoes in desolate rooms,
I cradle the pain, I cradle the shame,
Each scar a reminder, each wound a name.

I wrestle with shadows, I grapple with fear,
The faces of torment, so painfully near,
They whisper of failures, they taunt with despair,
Yet in their cold grip, I find strength to dare.

For in the abyss, where the heart learns to bleed,
I gather the pieces, I plant every seed,
With each tear that falls, a new bloom will rise,
From the ashes of sorrow, a phoenix will fly.

I confront the reflections, the truths I despise,
The lies that have shackled, the masks and the ties,
I scream into silence, I howl at the night,
In the depths of my shadow, I find my own light.

So here in the darkness, I learn to embrace,
The beauty in chaos, the strength in the grace,
For every demon I battle, every wound that I mend,
Is a step toward the light, a journey to transcend.

And though the path is heavy, the burden is real,
In the heart of the struggle, I learn how to heal,
With each breath I take, I reclaim what is mine,
In the depths of my shadow, my spirit will shine.

So let the tears flow, let the heartache be known,
For in the raw honesty, true courage is grown,
In the dance with the darkness, I find my own song,
In the depths of my shadow, I finally belong.

Let Me Be Clear

Let me be clear, I've walked through the fire,
With ashes of silence, and dreams that conspire,
For years I let shadows creep into my soul,
Worn down by the weight, I lost all control.

I wore the mask of peace, a fragile disguise,
While daggers of laughter cut deep from your eyes,
You smiled in my face, but your heart was a storm,
Innocent jabs wrapped in a venomous form.

I was the keeper of calm, the bearer of grace,
But in the stillness, I lost my own place,
I let you define me, I let you decide,
What love should look like, what pain I should hide.

But now, oh now, the tide has turned,
With boundaries erected, the lessons I've learned,
You don't get to talk down, you don't get to scorn,
I rise from the ashes, reborn and adorned.

I've tasted the bitterness, I've swallowed the lies,
I've danced with the demons that wore my disguise,
But in the depths of despair, I found my own voice,
A symphony of strength, a powerful choice.

I deserve the love that I give without end,
The warmth of my heart, the hand of a friend,
No longer a vessel for your cruel games,
I reclaim my spirit, I extinguish your flames.

I'm alert to the shade, I see through the guise,
The truth in your laughter, the hate in your eyes,
I've healed through the struggle, I've risen from pain,
With every step forward, I break every chain.

So let me be clear, I stand tall and proud,
No longer a whisper, I shout it aloud,
Respect is the currency I demand in return,
For the love that I give, for the lessons I've learned.

So tread lightly around me, for I've found my own way,
In the garden of healing, I blossom each day,
With roots deep in courage, and branches that soar,
I'm no longer your puppet, I'm so much more.

Let the tears fall like rain, let the heartache be known,
For in the raw honesty, my true self has grown,
In the battle with shadows, I've conquered the night,
Let me be clear: I am my own light.

Paradox of the Heart

In the quiet corners of a shattered soul,
Where shadows dance and whispers toll,
One thing I've learned, a truth so stark,
Life is a paradox, a haunting arc.

To heal, we must first embrace the pain,
Like rain that falls to nourish the grain,
Each tear a river, each scar a song,
In the depths of sorrow, we learn to belong.

To love, we must break open wide,
Expose the tender, the raw, the inside,
For love is a fire that burns and sears,
A beautiful chaos, igniting our fears.

In the heart's dark chamber, demons reside,
They claw and they gnash, they twist and they bide,
Yet in their fierce grip, we find our might,
For battling shadows reveals the light.

Never regret the paths that you tread,
Each stumble, each fall, each word left unsaid,
For every experience, a lesson bestowed,
In the soil of anguish, our spirits are sowed.

The weight of the world can crush the chest,
A heart heavy-laden, seeking its rest,
But in the chaos, a whisper will rise,
A promise of dawn, a glimpse of the skies.

So let the tears flow, let the heart break,
For in every fracture, new strength we make,
The light always follows, a beacon so bright,
Guiding us home through the depths of the night.

Embrace the paradox, the joy and the strife,
For in every ending, there's a spark of new life,
And though we may falter, though we may fall,
In the tapestry woven, we're part of it all.

So stand in the storm, let the winds howl and scream,
For beyond the tempest lies the sweetest dream,
A heart that has battled, a soul that has soared,
In the paradox of life, we are forever restored.

Sanctuary of Sweat

In the heart of the city, where shadows collide,
There lies a sanctuary, where dreams dare to bide,
The gym is a special place, a refuge, a home,
Unbiased and reliable, where lost souls can roam.

It doesn't care what burdens you bear,
What storms rage inside, what weight you wear,
It welcomes the weary, the broken, the bruised,
In its embrace, the chaos is diffused.

Here, the echoes of life fade to a whisper,
As you step through the door, the world grows crisper,
The clank of the weights, a symphony of strife,
Each rep a reminder of the battle for life.

The sweat drips like rain from a sky full of pain,
Each drop a testament to the struggle, the strain,
The sacrifice etched in the lines of your skin,
A canvas of courage, where the journey begins.

You push through the limits, the doubts, and the fears,
With every heartbeat, you silence the tears,
For in this arena, you're not just a ghost,
You're forging a warrior, the one you'll love most.

The excruciating effort, the fire in your chest,
Is a promise to rise, to become your best,
To shed the old self, the shadows that cling,
And embrace the potential that hope dares to bring.

In the mirror, reflections of who you could be,
A vision emerging, a glimpse of the free,
The person you're meant to be, waiting in line,
As you sculpt your existence, one rep at a time.

So let the world outside rage, let it howl and scream,
In this sacred space, you're living the dream,
For here, in the struggle, you find your true worth,
In the sanctuary of sweat, you're reborn from the earth.

And when the last set is done, when the lights start to fade,
You'll carry the strength, the resolve that you've made,
For the gym is a mirror, reflecting your fight,
A testament to darkness, transformed into light.

So weep for the battles, for the scars that you bear,
For the moments of doubt, for the weight of despair,
But know in this journey, you're never alone,
In the gym's quiet embrace, you've finally found home.

What If

What if the part of who we are,
That tender thread, that beating scar,
Went with them to heaven's light,
Leaving us in endless night?

What if laughter, once our song,
Now echoes hollow, feels so wrong?
The jokes we shared, the dreams we spun,
Now haunt the silence, one by one.

What if the warmth of their embrace,
Is lost in time, a vanished trace?
The whispered secrets, the midnight calls,
Now linger like shadows on empty walls.

What if the colours of our days,
Turned to grey in a cruel haze?
The world feels heavy, the air is thick,
Each breath a reminder, a heart-wrenching trick.

What if the memories, once so bright,
Are now just ghosts in the fading light?
The laughter we shared, the tears we cried,
Now drown in sorrow, where love has died.

What if the part of us that shines,
Is buried deep in the cruel designs,
Of fate that took them, swift and cold,
Leaving us with a story untold?

What if the dreams we dared to weave,
Are now just threads we can't believe?
The future we painted, now torn apart,
A canvas of grief, a shattered heart.

What if the love that we once knew,
Is lost in the echoes of "I miss you"?
Each day a battle, each night a fight,
To find a way to make it right.

What if the part of us that's gone,
Is the very piece that keeps us strong?
Yet here we stand, in the wake of despair,
Searching for solace, but finding air.

What if the stars that once burned bright,
Now flicker dimly in the endless night?
We carry their spirit, we hold them near,
Yet every heartbeat reminds us they're not here.

What if the part of who we are,
Is forever lost, a distant star?
In the silence, we scream, in the darkness, we cry,
For the friend we lost, for the love that won't die.

What if the part of us that remains,
Is a testament to love, through all the pain?
Though they've gone to a place we can't see,
In our hearts, they live on, eternally free.

The Cost of Shadows: A Journey to Light

In the quiet of the night, when the world is still,
A whisper called my name, a haunting, bitter thrill.
It wrapped around my heart, a serpent cold and sly,
With every breath I took, I felt the demons sigh.

They danced upon my shoulders, with laughter sharp as knives,
Each promise that they offered, a thousand shattered lives.
They painted dreams in colours, vibrant, wild, and bright,
But in the morning's light, they faded, consumed by night.

I chased the fleeting moments, the highs that burned like fire,
But every spark ignited chains, a bond that pulled me higher.
I wore a mask of joy, but underneath it lay the truth,
A hollow shell of memories, the ghost of my lost youth.

I fought the battles bravely, with fists clenched tight in rage,
But every victory I claimed, I found I was still a cage.
The chains of sweet addiction rattled deep within my soul,
Each link a bitter memory, each weight a heavy toll.

I saw the faces of my loved ones, their eyes a well of pain,
They reached for me in silence, but I was lost in disdain.
I turned my back on laughter, on warmth, on love's embrace,
In the mirror's cruel reflection, I saw a stranger's face.

The nights stretched long and endless, a void I could not fill,
With every sip, each fleeting hit, I lost a piece of will.
The laughter turned to echoes, the joy to bitter tears,
And in the depths of darkness, I confronted all my fears.

Oh, how I longed for freedom, to break these chains that bind,
To silence all the whispers, to leave the past behind.
But every step I took felt like a step into the fire,
A dance with all my demons, a waltz of lost desire.

I stumbled through the shadows, three times I fell to ground,
Each failure carved a deeper wound, each loss a heavier sound.
But in the depths of sorrow, a flicker sparked anew,
A whisper of redemption, a chance to break on through.

The fourth time felt like magic, a shift within my core,
With trembling hands, I reached for hope, a light I could restore.
I stood upon the precipice, the edge of all I knew,
And with a heart wide open, I chose to start anew.

The journey wasn't easy; the road was long and steep,
But every tear I shed became a promise I would keep.
With every day of clarity, I felt the weight release,
The chains that once had bound me began to fall in peace.

I found the strength in struggle, the pride in every scar,
For in the fight for freedom, I learned just who we are.
The shadows that once haunted me now danced in distant light,
And in the heart of battle, I discovered my own might.

So here I stand, a warrior, with scars that tell my tale,
A heart that's bruised and battered, yet still I will not fail.
For in the depths of sorrow, I found a way to rise,
A glimmer of redemption, a phoenix in the skies.

Let the world bear witness, let the tears fall like rain,
For in the heart of struggle, there's beauty in the pain.
The price of sweet addiction was steep, but I have paid,
And in the light of freedom, I stand unafraid.

With pride that swells within me, I wear my truth like gold,
For every step I've taken, a story to be told.
The cost of shadows taught me, through darkness I have grown,
And in the light of healing, I've finally found my home.

Unapologetically Me:
A Symphony of One

In a world of echoes, where shadows often blend,
I stand, a solitary note, a truth that will not bend.
A tapestry of colours, woven from my scars,
Each thread a whispered secret, each mark a dance with stars.

I've walked through fields of judgment, where whispers cut like glass,
Where mirrors held reflections of a self I dared not pass.
They told me to conform, to fit within their mold,
But I was born a wildfire, a spirit fierce and bold.

I've battled with the demons that lurked beneath my skin,
Their voices dripped with poison, their laughter steeped in sin.
They tried to steal my essence, to drown my vibrant hue,
But in the depths of darkness, I found the strength to break through.

I've tasted bitter failure, I've danced with doubt and fear,
Each stumble carved a lesson, each tear a badge I wear.
I've fought the tides of silence, the weight of heavy chains,
And in the storm of struggle, I learned to dance in rain.

Oh, how the world can shatter, how hearts can break in two,
When all you seek is solace, a place to just be you.
But in the cracks of sorrow, I found a light so bright,
A spark that whispered softly, "You are your own delight."

I am the song of thunder, the whisper of the breeze,
The laughter of the wildflowers that sway beneath the trees.
I am the storm and stillness, the chaos and the calm,
A symphony of contradictions, a heart that beats like a psalm.

I wear my truth like armour, each flaw a precious gem,
For in the depths of struggle, I've learned to love my stem.
I am the scars of battles fought, the courage in my veins,
The beauty in my brokenness, the joy that still remains.

I am the voice of silence, the roar of quiet grace,
The one who stands unyielding, who dares to take up space.
I am the fire that flickers, the phoenix rising high,
A testament to living, to loving, to the why.

So let the world bear witness, let the tears fall like rain,
For in the heart of struggle, there's beauty in the pain.
I am unapologetic, a force that cannot break,
A melody of courage, a truth that I will stake.

With every breath I take, I claim my rightful place,
A unique and shining spirit, a soul that's full of grace.
I am the laughter echoing in the depths of darkest night,
A beacon of authenticity, a heart that's pure and bright.

So here I stand, unyielding, a masterpiece of one,
A canvas painted boldly, beneath the blazing sun.
For I am not a whisper; I am the thunder's call,
A symphony of one, and I will rise, I will not fall.

In the tapestry of life, I weave my own design,
With threads of joy and sorrow, I claim this heart of mine.
For I am one of a kind, a truth that's fierce and free,
And in the depths of my existence, I am unapologetically me.

Chapters of Strength

In the quiet shadows where whispers dwell,
Your scars tell stories, a haunting spell.
Not chains that bind, but pages turned,
In the book of your life, where courage burned.

Each mark a testament, a battle fought,
A silent echo of the lessons taught.
They trace the paths of your darkest nights,
Yet in their depths, a flicker ignites.

You wore the weight of a thousand fears,
Each tear a river, each sigh a year.
But listen closely, hear the refrain,
From the ashes of sorrow, you rise again.

Break free from the trauma, let the past fade,
Step boldly into the light, unafraid.
For every wound is a seed of grace,
A reminder that healing is not a race.

In the dawn of your new beginning,
Feel the warmth of hope, the joy of winning.
The sun will kiss the scars on your skin,
And whisper softly, "You are not your sin."

So gather your strength, let the world see,
The beauty in struggle, the power to be.
For in every chapter, both dark and bright,
You are the author, you are the light.

And when the tears fall, let them flow free,
For they water the roots of your destiny.
Embrace the journey, the highs and the lows,
In the garden of life, your spirit still grows.

So stand tall, dear heart, let your story unfold,
In the tapestry woven, your truth will be told.
Your scars are not chains; they're the strength you possess,
A symphony of survival, a testament to bless.

To My Princess, My Light

In the quiet of night, when shadows creep,
I wrestle with demons that steal my sleep.
Cancer, a thief, with its cold, cruel hand,
Has drawn a dark line in the life I had planned.

At thirty-four, I stand on this precipice,
With a heart full of love, yet drowning in abyss.
How do I tell you, my sweet, tender girl,
That the world as you know it is about to unfurl?

Your laughter, your dreams, your bright, shining eyes,
Are the stars in my sky, the sun in my rise.
But now, as I face this relentless despair,
I'm haunted by visions of moments we'll share.

I wanted to see you in your prom dress,
To twirl you around, to witness your best.
To cheer as you conquer each challenge and test,
To cradle your dreams, to love you, to rest.

Yet here I am, with a cough that betrays,
Each breath a reminder of life's cruel ways.
I taste the iron, the blood, the decay,
And I fear for your heart, for the price you must pay.

How can I burden you with this weight?
A child should not carry the fear of such fate.
You've weathered the storms, you've fought through the pain,
And now I must tell you, I'm caught in the rain.

But listen, my darling, my angel, my light,
In the depths of this darkness, I'll continue to fight.
For you are my reason, my strength, my refrain,
In the battle of battles, I'll rise up again.

I'll teach you of courage, of love that won't fade,
Of standing for truth, of the choices we've made.
Though the shadows may linger, and the nights may be long,
Know that in my heart, you will always belong.

So if the worst comes, if I'm called to the skies,
Remember my love, it will never say goodbye.
You are my heartbeat, my breath, my sweet song,
In the tapestry of life, you've made me so strong.

I'll whisper my love through the winds and the trees,
In the rustle of leaves, in the soft summer breeze.
You'll carry my spirit, my hopes, and my dreams,
And together we'll conquer, or so it seems.

For in every tear, in each moment of strife,
You'll find the resilience that colours your life.
And though I may falter, I'll never let go,
For my love is a river, forever will flow.

So stand tall, my princess, with your head held high,
You are my forever, my reason to try.
In the face of the darkness, we'll find our own way,
Together, my darling, we'll seize every day.

And when the dawn breaks, with its golden embrace,
Know that I'm with you, in every new place.
For love knows no bounds, it transcends time and space,
In the heart of my angel, I've found my true grace.

Echoes of Connection

In the quiet corners of a world so loud,
Where shadows dance beneath a heavy shroud,
There walks a soul, tender and bare,
An empath, cradling the weight of despair.

With eyes like oceans, deep and wide,
They feel the pulse of the earth, the pain inside,
Each heartbeat a story, each sigh a plea,
In the silence of nature, they find their decree.

A wounded bird, with feathers askew,
Lies trembling softly, its spirit askew,
With gentle hands, the empath draws near,
Whispering solace, erasing the fear.

"Dear friend," they murmur, "you're not alone,
In this vast universe, you've found a home.
I'll carry your sorrow, I'll share in your flight,
Together we'll rise, through the dark into light."

A stray dog, with eyes like pools of regret,
Hides in the shadows, a heart full of debt,
The empath kneels down, their heart in their hands,
And the dog feels the warmth of love's gentle strands.

"Your past is a burden, but here you are free,
In the tapestry of life, you're woven with me.
Let's chase the horizon, let's dance in the rain,
For every lost moment, we'll gather the pain."

In the depths of the forest, where the wild things roam,
The empath finds solace, a place to call home,
With each creature they meet, a bond forged in tears,
A symphony of heartbeats, a chorus of fears.

But the world is a tempest, cruel and unkind,
And the empath, they carry the weight of mankind,
For every lost soul, every cry in the night,
They bear the burden, they fight the good fight.

Yet in the stillness, when the stars start to weep,
They feel the connection, a promise to keep,
For every soft whimper, every gentle nudge,
Is a reminder of love, a sacred pledge.

But oh, the heart aches, as the seasons must change,
As the wild ones grow weary, their spirits estranged,
The empath stands watch, as the shadows descend,
Knowing each farewell is a heart that must bend.

With tears like rivers, they whisper goodbye,
To the souls they have loved, to the spirits that fly,
And in that moment, the world feels so vast,
As they gather the memories, the echoes of past.

For in every connection, in every embrace,
Lies the truth of existence, the beauty of grace,
Though the heart may be heavy, and the journey is long,
In the arms of the wild, they forever belong.

So let the tears flow, let the heartache be known,
For the empath and animals, together have grown,
In a world that is aching, they find their own way,
In the whispers of love, they'll forever stay.

Inside You, the World

You are beginning to understand,
Aren't you?
That the whole world is inside you,
A universe of whispers,
Echoes of laughter and tears,
In the chambers of your heart,
Where shadows dance with light,
And every heartbeat is a story,
Every breath a silent prayer.

To find peace, you must first embrace
The tempest within,
The chaos that churns,
The doubts that claw at your spirit,
For in the storm, you are forged,
In the fire of your own making,
You learn to rise,
To stand tall amidst the ruins,
To gather the fragments of your soul,
And weave them into a tapestry of strength.

To truly enjoy life,
You must savour the essence of who you are,
The scars that map your journey,
The laughter that spills like sunlight,
The tears that carve rivers of resilience,
For in the depths of your being,
You hold the key to joy,
A treasure buried beneath the weight of the world,
Waiting for you to unearth it,
To dance in the rain of your own making,
To sing the song only you can hear.

And once you learn to master this,
To cradle your spirit in gentle hands,
You will be shielded from the storms,
From the whispers that tell you,
You are not enough,
That the world is too heavy to bear.
For with this gift of recognising yourself,
You will find that even in solitude,
You are never truly alone.

In the quiet moments,
When the world fades to a whisper,
You will hear the symphony of your heart,
The melody of your existence,
A chorus of dreams and hopes,
That rise like phoenixes from the ashes,
And in that sacred space,
You will discover the truth:
You are the universe,
And the universe is you.

So let the tears fall,
Let them cleanse the wounds,
For in the shedding of sorrow,
You will find the seeds of joy,
And in the embrace of your own spirit,
You will learn to soar,
To dance with the stars,
To hold the world in your hands,
And know,
You are enough.
You are everything.
You are home.

A Mother's Heart

If you asked me about my mum,
I'd smile, say she's nice and funny,
Her laughter dances like sunlight,
A melody that warms the coldest days.
But if you dared to look deeper,
To peel back the layers of her soul,
I'd falter, my voice a whisper,
And tears would spill like rain on parched earth.

For she is a tapestry woven with scars,
Each thread a story of battles fought,
Of nights spent wrestling with shadows,
Of dreams deferred, yet never forgotten.
I've watched her, a warrior in silence,
Her heart a fortress, yet tender as spring,
Bearing burdens that would crush lesser souls,
Yet rising, always rising, like the dawn.

I've seen her struggle,
Her tears like rivers carving canyons,
Each drop a testament to her strength,
Each sob a prayer for brighter tomorrows.
In the quiet of the night,
When the world slumbers,
I've heard her heart break,
Yet still, she gathers the pieces,
Crafting love from the fragments of despair.

She fought for me with a fierceness,
A lioness guarding her cub,
Through storms that threatened to drown us,
Through darkness that whispered defeat.
And still, she stood,
A lighthouse in my tempest,
Guiding me home with her unwavering light,
Her love a balm for my weary spirit.

Oh, how she carries the weight of the world,
Yet finds the strength to lift me higher,
To teach me that love is a battle worth fighting,
That hope is a flame that never dies.
In her embrace, I find my refuge,
In her laughter, I find my joy,
For she is the strongest woman in my eyes,
A testament to resilience, a symphony of grace.

So if you ask me about my mum,
Know that beneath the surface,
Lies a universe of courage and sacrifice,
A heart that beats with the rhythm of love.
And as I stand here, tears streaming,
I celebrate her, the warrior, the nurturer,
For in her, I see the essence of life,
A love so profound, it echoes through eternity.

And when the world feels heavy,
When shadows threaten to consume,
I'll carry her spirit within me,
A legacy of strength, a beacon of hope.
For she is my heart, my home, my everything,
And in her love, I find the power to rise,
To face the storms, to embrace the light,
For she is my mother, my hero, my soul.

From Shadows to Light

In the heart of Brisbane, where the city hums,
I danced with demons, my soul weighed down,
Seven years in the grip of a merciless vice,
A needle's kiss, a pipe's cruel embrace,
Each hit a promise, each promise a lie,
I chased the dragon, but it left me to die.

In the beginning, it felt like flight,
A rush of euphoria, a spark in the night,
But soon the high turned to chains,
A prison of pleasure, a cycle of pain.
I wore my addiction like a second skin,
A mask of false joy, a battle within.

I remember the nights, the whispers of despair,
The hollow laughter, the vacant stare,
Each moment a struggle, each breath a fight,
In the depths of the darkness, I lost all my light.
I fought with my demons, they clawed at my mind,
In the silence of shadows, I was left far behind.

Suicide lingered, a ghost at my side,
A siren's call, a dark, twisted guide,
I stood on the edge, with nothing to lose,
But a flicker of hope whispered, "You choose."
So I took a step back, a breath in the night,
And in that small moment, I chose to fight.

Then came Tamworth, a whisper of change,
A chance to rebuild, to break from the chains,
With trembling hands, I let go of the past,
Each day a new battle, each moment a task.
I faced the abyss, the pain I had sown,
And slowly, like dawn, I began to feel grown.

Five hundred days, a milestone of grace,
Each sunrise a victory, each heartbeat a trace,
Of the strength I discovered, the love I reclaimed,
From the ashes of sorrow, a new life was named.
I learned to forgive the boy lost in the haze,
To honour the struggle, to cherish the days.

The road was not easy, the scars still remain,
But I wear them with pride, a map of my pain.
I've danced with the darkness, I've tasted the night,
Yet here I stand, a survivor, a light.
From the depths of despair to the heights of my dreams,
I've woven my story from heartache and seams.

Now I breathe in the beauty, the colours, the sound,
The laughter of children, the love all around.
I've learned to embrace every moment, each tear,
For they've shaped who I am, they've brought me right here.
From the needle to the pipe, from shadows to sun,
I've fought for my life, and I've finally won.

So if you see me, know I'm not just a face,
I'm a testament to courage, to love, and to grace.
For every soul lost, for every heart torn,
I carry their stories, their battles, their scorn.
And in my journey, I find strength to share,
That hope is a flame, and love is the air.

From the brink of despair to the promise of dawn,
I rise like the phoenix, reborn and withdrawn.
Five hundred days clean, a warrior's embrace,
I stand here, alive, in this beautiful space.
So let the tears flow, let the heartache be known,
For in every struggle, we're never alone.

One Life

You have this one life, a fragile thread,
Woven with whispers of dreams, and echoes of words left unsaid.
How do you want to spend it, in shadows of doubt,
Apologising for the light that flickers within,
Or regretting the moments you let slip away,
Like grains of sand through fingers that fray?

Do you want to question the worth of your heart,
To hate the reflection that tears you apart?
To diet on sorrow, to run after ghosts,
Who don't see your beauty, who don't know your hopes?

Be brave, dear soul, let courage ignite,
For the world needs your fire, your laughter, your light.
Believe in yourself, let the chains fall away,
Embrace every heartbeat, each breath, every day.

Take risks, take chances, let your spirit take flight,
For life is a canvas, paint it bold, paint it bright.
You have this one life, don't let it slip by,
Make yourself proud, let your spirit soar high.

But oh, the weight of the choices, the burden of fear,
The haunting of moments that never drew near.
The love that you lost, the words left unspoken,
The dreams that you buried, the promises broken.

So gather your courage, let the tears fall like rain,
For each drop is a story, a testament to pain.
And in that raw beauty, in the ache of your heart,
You'll find the strength to make a new start.

You have this one life, let it not be in vain,
For the scars that you carry are proof of your gain.
So rise from the ashes, let your spirit be free,
And know that your journey is a gift to the sea.

Make waves with your laughter, let your heart be your guide,
For in this one life, you are meant to collide
With the beauty of living, the joy of the fight,
And the love that surrounds you, in the dark and the light.

So weep for the moments that slipped through your hands,
But dance for the future, for the dreams yet to land.
You have this one life, let it echo your name,
And in the end, may you never feel shame.

For you are a warrior, a beacon, a flame,
And in this one life, you'll never be the same.

A Glimpse of Blue

In the realm where shadows loom,
Where thunder rumbles, and sorrows bloom,
You see the tempest, the stormy night,
But I, I search for a flicker of light.

You gaze at the clouds, heavy and grey,
The weight of the world in disarray,
Yet in that corner, where darkness seems vast,
I find a whisper, a promise to last.

A tiny blue patch, a sliver so small,
A beacon of hope amidst the squall,
While you drown in the depths of despair,
I cling to that azure, that breath of fresh air.

You call it denial, a trick of the mind,
But in that small fragment, true strength I find,
For life is a canvas, both dark and divine,
And I choose to paint with the colours that shine.

The storms may rage, the winds may howl,
But I'll dance in the rain, I'll embrace every scowl,
For every tempest that threatens to break,
I'll hold to that blue, for my own heart's sake.

You see the chaos, the pain, the dread,
But I see the dawn, the light that's ahead,
In the heart of the storm, I find my refrain,
A symphony woven from joy and from pain.

So when you ask how my mind can endure,
Know that I'm searching for something more pure,
In the darkest of nights, I'll find my way through,
For I am the dreamer who lives for the blue.

And though tears may fall like the rain from the sky,
I'll gather each drop, let them nourish my sigh,
For in every heartache, in every lost fight,
There's a glimmer of hope, a flicker of light.

So weep if you must, let the sorrow unfold,
But remember the blue, the warmth to behold,
For in every storm, there's a promise anew,
And I'll keep on believing, in the power of blue.

Remember

In the quiet corners of your heart,
Where dreams whisper softly, yet tear apart,
When the world spins wild, and the nights grow long,
Remember, dear soul, where you truly belong.

When the laughter of friends feels hollow and thin,
And the echoes of parties drown out the din,
When the glitter and glamour fade into dust,
Remember your purpose, your passion, your trust.

For the 1% club is not for the faint,
It's a sanctuary built for the brave and the saint,
Where goals rise like phoenixes, fierce and bright,
In the shadows of doubt, they ignite the night.

So gather your courage, let the fire burn,
In the depths of your struggle, it's your turn to learn,
That the path may be rugged, the journey may sting,
But the weight of your dreams is a powerful thing.

When the world tries to pull you into its sway,
And the sirens of comfort beg you to stay,
Remember the vision that dances in sight,
The life you've imagined, the future so bright.

For every tear shed is a seed in the ground,
A testament forged in the silence profound,
And the pain that you carry, the burdens you bear,
Are the wings of your spirit, the strength in your prayer.

So rise, oh brave heart, let your spirit take flight,
With the fire of purpose, you'll conquer the night,
For the 1% club is a call to the bold,
A promise of greatness, a story retold.

Remember, dear dreamer, the power you hold,
In the depths of your struggle, let your truth unfold,
When your goals are your compass, your heart is your guide,
You'll find in the journey, the strength to abide.

So stand up, take action, let your voice be heard,
In the symphony of life, let your passion be stirred,
For the world needs your light, your courage, your grace,
Remember, dear soul, you're destined to chase.

In the tapestry woven with threads of your fight,
You'll inspire the weary to rise with delight,
So remember, remember, when the night feels so long,
Your goals are your anthem, your heart is your song.

Fragments of a Shattered Soul

In the quiet corners of a once-bright heart,
Where laughter danced like sunlight, now shadows depart,
You stand before me, a ghost of your past,
A tapestry of joy unravelled, threads cast.

I hardly recognise the light in your eyes,
Once a beacon of hope, now a veil of goodbyes,
You've changed, my friend, like the seasons in flight,
From vibrant blooms to the chill of the night.

What do you mean? The words tremble, they ache,
A fragile façade, a heart ready to break,
You ask for the truth, and I wish I could lie,
But the weight of your sorrow is too heavy to deny.

You're broken now, a puzzle with pieces misplaced,
Each fragment a memory, a smile now erased,
When I see you, I see the echoes of pain,
A canvas of anguish, washed over by rain.

You used to be carefree, a spirit unchained,
Now you walk on the edge, where hope is constrained,
The laughter that once filled the air like a song,
Is now but a whisper, where did it go wrong?

Demons dance in the shadows, they whisper your name,
They feast on your fears, igniting the flame,
Each heartbeat a battle, each breath a despair,
You wear your scars like armour, but they're heavy to bear.

I see the cracks in your smile, the tremor in your voice,
The silence that lingers, the absence of choice,
You're a warrior, yes, but the war has been long,
And the echoes of sorrow drown out your song.

So let me hold your heart, let me cradle your pain,
In the depths of this darkness, let's find light again,
For even in brokenness, beauty can bloom,
In the ashes of anguish, let love find its room.

Together we'll gather the pieces you've lost,
We'll weave them with hope, no matter the cost,
For in the depths of despair, a flicker remains,
A promise of healing, a chance to break chains.

So let the tears fall, let them wash you anew,
For in every drop lies the strength to break through,
You're not just a shadow, you're more than this fight,
You're a soul that can rise, a phoenix in flight.

And though the road's heavy, and the night feels so long,
Remember, dear friend, you are never alone,
For I'll stand beside you, through darkness and strife,
Together we'll mend what was shattered in life.

The Echo of Loss

In the stillness of dawn, when the world holds its breath,
I wake to the shadows, the whispers of death.
Your laughter, a ghost that dances in air,
A haunting reminder of love laid bare.

The sun rises slowly, yet it feels like a curse,
Each ray a reminder, each moment a verse,
Of a life that was vibrant, now muted and grey,
In the silence, I search for the words left to say.

Society smiles, with its well-meaning lies,
"Time heals all wounds," they say, with bright eyes.
But they don't know the demons that claw at my soul,
The ache of your absence, the gaping, deep hole.

They don't see the nights when the tears fall like rain,
When the weight of your memory is both pleasure and pain.
Each heartbeat a reminder, each breath a cruel test,
Of a love that was boundless, now laid to rest.

I wear my grief like a shroud, heavy and tight,
A cloak of despair that swallows the light.
Yet in this dark journey, I find pieces of me,
In the fragments of sorrow, I begin to see.

For every day that passes, I'm further away,
From the warmth of your smile, the words you would say.
But with each sunset's glow, I feel you draw near,
In the whispers of twilight, your spirit is clear.

There's no end date for grief, no finish line drawn,
Just a path that I walk, where the shadows are long.
And though the world moves on, with its hurried embrace,
I linger in moments, in the stillness of space.

I've learned that healing is not a straight road,
It's a winding, wild journey, a heavy, sweet load.
Some days I am shattered, some days I am whole,
But through every fracture, I reclaim my soul.

So I'll honour your memory, in the tears that I shed,
In the laughter that bubbles, in the words left unsaid.
For love doesn't vanish; it transforms and it grows,
In the garden of grief, where the wildflower knows.

And though I may stumble, and though I may fall,
I'll rise from the ashes, I'll answer the call.
For you are my compass, my light in the dark,
In the depths of my sorrow, you've left your mark.

So here's to the journey, the pain and the grace,
To the love that remains, in this sacred space.
For every heartbeat echoes, a testament true,
That grief is a river, and I'll flow on through.

In the tapestry woven with threads of our days,
I'll carry your spirit in countless ways.
And though I may ache, and the world may not see,
In the depths of my heart, you'll forever be free.

In the Echoes of a Child's Heart

In the cradle of a country torn apart,
A child stood witness, a trembling heart,
Civil war raged, a tempest of pain,
Innocence shattered, like glass in the rain.

He watched as the shadows swallowed the light,
As families fractured in the dead of night,
With every explosion, a piece of him fell,
In the silence that followed, he learned to dwell.

Years rolled on, and the boy became man,
But the scars of his childhood, they shaped who he ran,
Through jungles of sorrow, he sought to be free,
Yet the chains of the past whispered, "You're not me."

In the grip of addiction, he stumbled and fell,
Overdosed on dreams, in a personal hell,
Each high a moment, a fleeting embrace,
But the crash that followed left a hollowed space.

Stabbed by betrayal, shot by disdain,
Beaten by life, yet he rose once again,
Each bruise a reminder of battles unseen,
Of a heart that kept fighting, though weary and lean.

In love's cruel arena, a marriage fell apart,
Promises broken, a fracture of heart,
Yet in the wreckage, he found a new role,
A single parent, with a fierce, tender soul.

With gentle hands, he cradled his child,
In a world that judged, so harsh and wild,
He whispered of strength, of love's endless grace,
"Your heart is your armour; you'll find your place."

But the world outside, it cast its stone,
"Not man enough," they sneered, "you're all alone."
Yet in his spirit, a fire burned bright,
A truth unyielding, a warrior's light.

Transmasculine, they said, as if it were sin,
But he wore his identity like a badge within,
For every label, a story to tell,
Of battles fought bravely, of rising from hell.

So here stands a man, not defined by the scars,
But by the love that he carries, the light of the stars,
In the tapestry woven with threads of his pain,
He finds his strength, he dances in rain.

Tear-jerking, soul-crushing, a life intertwined,
In the heart of a child, a spirit refined,
For in every struggle, in every dark night,
He's a beacon of hope, a testament of light.

So weep for the battles, the losses, the strife,
But celebrate the courage that breathes in his life,
For he is enough, in a world so unkind,
A warrior, a mother, a heart intertwined.

The Weight of Shadows

In the quiet of the night, when the world is still,
A whisper calls my name, a promise to fulfil.
It dances on the edge of reason, a siren's sweet embrace,
A fleeting glimpse of heaven, in this desolate place.

I chase the ghost of solace, a fleeting, fragile high,
With trembling hands, I reach for it, as the demons laugh nearby.
They know my every weakness, they know my every fear,
They wrap around my heart like chains, and draw me ever near.

Each hit, a fleeting moment, a spark that lights the dark,
But when the fire flickers out, I'm left with just a mark.
A hollowed shell of who I was, a shadow of my soul,
The echoes of my laughter fade, as I pay the toll.

I wear the scars of battles fought, the wounds that never heal,
Each promise made, each vow I broke, a truth I cannot feel.
I stand upon the precipice, where hope and sorrow meet,
And in the depths of silence, I hear my own heart beat.

The high, it comes like thunder, a storm that shakes the ground,
But when the clouds disperse, I'm lost, nowhere to be found.
The euphoria, a fleeting kiss, a lover's cruel deceit,
And when it leaves, I'm left alone, with shadows at my feet.

I claw at walls of memory, where joy once used to dwell,
But now they're painted over with the colours of my hell.
I see the faces of the ones I love, their eyes a mirror's pain,
And in their gaze, I find the truth: I'm dancing in the rain.

Each drop a bitter reminder of the life I used to know,
A garden once of laughter, now a graveyard of my woe.
I wear my addiction like a shroud, a cloak of endless night,
And in the depths of darkness, I search for one last light.

But the light is just a flicker, a candle in the storm,
And as I reach to grasp it, I feel the shadows swarm.
They pull me back to madness, to the cycle I can't break,
And in the grip of longing, I lose more than I take.

So here I stand, a prisoner, in a cell of my own making,
With every breath, I'm suffocating, my heart forever aching.
I long for liberation, for a chance to start anew,
But the chains of my addiction are the only truth I knew.

And as the dawn approaches, with its cruel and bitter light,
I face the day with trembling hands, and a heart that's lost the fight.
For in the depths of silence, where the shadows softly creep,
I find the weight of shadows is a burden I must keep.

Life's Cruel Curriculum

Life, you love the way you teach me things, don't you?
With a smile that cuts like glass,
You hand me lessons wrapped in heartache,
Each one a dagger, each one a mask.

"Here, Dex," you whisper,
"Fall for this person, let your heart ignite,
Now learn to let go, to sever the tether,
To watch the stars dim in the night."

You watch as I tumble,
Into the depths of love's sweet embrace,
Only to rise, a ghost of my former self,
In the hollow echo of her space.

"Live here," you taunt,
"Where laughter once danced in the air,
Where memories linger like shadows,
And joy is a ghost, a cruel snare."

I swear you smoke the fattest one,
When you weave your web of despair,
You laugh as I drown in nostalgia,
As I choke on the weight of the air.

I know I'm destined for one of humanity's highest callings,
To wear the crown of suffering, to bear the weight,
To feel the sharp edges of love's cruel lessons,
To learn that joy often comes with a heavy fate.

You teach me strength through the cracks in my heart,
Through the nights spent wrestling with shadows and fears,
You mold me in fire, in sorrow, in pain,
As I gather the shards of my shattered years.

But oh, how I ache for the moments we shared,
For the laughter that echoed, the warmth of her smile,
Yet here I stand, a soldier of grief,
Marching through memories, mile after mile.

If you want to be stronger, you say,
Life will put you through trials, through storms,
But what of the heart that's been shattered,
What of the soul that no longer warms?

I know I'm on the right path,
Because life has turned cruel, it's true,
But in this darkness, I search for the light,
For the strength to rise, to start anew.

So teach me, Life, with your merciless hand,
With your lessons that cut and your trials that burn,
For in this suffering, I'll find my way,
And from these ashes, I will learn.

But know this, dear Life, as I walk through the fire,
Each tear that I shed is a testament,
To the love that I lost, to the dreams that expire,
And in this heartache, I find my lament.

So let the world weep with me,
Let the skies rain down their sorrow,
For in this pain, I'll carve my truth,
And rise from the depths, to face tomorrow.

Resilient Heart

In the shadows where whispers dwell,
I've fed the mouths that cursed my name,
With every bite, a silent spell,
A dance of love wrapped in their shame.

I've wiped the tears from faces cold,
Those who've carved my heart with knives,
Yet still, I gather strength untold,
In the wreckage, my spirit thrives.

I've lifted souls from depths of night,
Those who sought to drag me down,
With every hand I've reached in fight,
I wore their burdens like a crown.

I've done the favours, given grace,
To those who'd turn and walk away,
In kindness, I've found my own embrace,
A light that guides me through the fray.

Crazy? Maybe, but here I stand,
A warrior forged in love and pain,
With scars that map this weary land,
I rise again, I break the chain.

I will not lose myself in spite,
Nor drown in hatred's bitter sea,
For in the dark, I find my light,
I am who I am, unapologetically.

Life isn't easy, it's a storm,
Yet through the chaos, I remain,
With every bruise, I've been reborn,
In every tear, I've found my flame.

So let them talk, let them conspire,
Their demons dance, but I won't bend,
For in my heart, a fierce desire,
To love, to heal, to never end.

I'll stand my ground, I'll face the fight,
With every breath, I claim my right,
To be the truth, to be the free,
To live my life, unapologetically me.

In the Mirror of Our Hearts

In the mirror of our hearts, reflections collide,
A world of shadows, where pain tries to hide.
You see her there, the girl with the weight,
Each step a battle, each breath a debate.

Her eyes cast down, a storm in her chest,
A warrior weary, in a world unblessed.
She feels the whispers, the judgmental stares,
A symphony of silence, a chorus of cares.

So if your gaze meets hers, let kindness ignite,
A smile, a beacon, in the depths of her night.
For every glance that cuts, every laugh that stings,
Is a dagger of doubt, that the darkness brings.

And what of the old man, lost in the fray,
Fumbling with machines, in a world gone grey?
You laugh with your friends, your phone in your hand,
But he's fighting his battles, alone, unplanned.

What if you paused, just a moment to see,
The courage it takes to be who he'd be?
Instead of the mockery, the snickers, the scorn,
Show him the way, let compassion be born.

And that gangly teen, with his awkward embrace,
Mirroring strength, in a desperate race.
He's not just a shadow, a copy, a fool,
He's a heart full of hope, in a world that's so cruel.

So let him be near, let him learn from your grace,
For admiration is love, not a reason to chase.
In the gym of our lives, we're all lifting weight,
Each burden we carry, each fear we create.

So pause for a moment, let empathy flow,
In the silence of struggle, let kindness bestow.
For we're all just reflections, in this fragile dance,
Each soul a story, each heart a chance.

And when you look closer, through the veil of disdain,
You'll see the humanity, the joy, and the pain.
In the mirror of our hearts, let compassion be found,
For the weight of our words can either lift or confound.

So smile at the girl, guide the man with the tool,
Embrace the young dreamer, let love be the rule.
For in this shared journey, we're all intertwined,
In the tapestry of life, let our hearts be aligned.

And when the tears fall, let them wash away shame,
For we're all just seeking, to be seen, to be named.
In the echoes of kindness, let our spirits take flight,
For the power of love can turn darkness to light.

The Price of Shadows

In the stillness of night, when the world holds its breath,
A battle rages on, a dance with death.
Whispers of demons, they claw at the mind,
A haunting reminder of the ties that bind.

Once a soul vibrant, with laughter and light,
Now a ghost in the mirror, lost in the fight.
He's not afraid of dying; it's living that haunts,
Each promise of solace, a dagger disguised,
A fleeting embrace, where hope is despised.

The price of addiction, a toll paid in tears,
A currency minted from anguish and fears.
With every small victory, a cost that is steep,
A heart once so full, now hollow and deep.

The needle, the bottle, the smoke in the air,
Each hit a reminder of the love that's not there.
A siren's sweet song, it lures and it taunts,
A lover so cruel, it steals what it wants.

In the daylight, they wear a mask of pretense,
But the shadows grow longer, the pain more intense.
They smile through the cracks, but the laughter is thin,
A fragile façade, where the darkness creeps in.

Each day is a war, with no end in sight,
A struggle for freedom, a fight for the light.
He rises from ashes, only to fall,
A phoenix in chains, answering addiction's call.

The nights stretch like rivers, with currents so strong,
Each wave a reminder of where he belongs.
In the depths of despair, he searches for way,
But the demons are hungry, and they're here to stay.

He's danced with the devil, he's tasted the fire,
Each moment a choice, each choice a desire.
But the cost of the high is a heart turned to stone,
A life once so vibrant, now shattered, alone.

And yet, in the silence, a flicker remains,
A whisper of hope, through the sorrow and chains.
For even in darkness, a spark can ignite,
A flicker of courage, a will to fight.

So here's to the warriors, the lost and the brave,
To the souls who are fighting, who long to be saved.
May you find your redemption, may you break free from the night,
For the dawn will come softly, bringing warmth, bringing light.

In the depths of addiction, let your spirit take flight,
For the price of the shadows is not worth the fight.
And though the road's heavy, and the journey is long,
Remember, dear heart, you are still so strong.

Home in the Heart:
A Journey to Acceptance

In shadows deep, where silence dwells,
A heart once bound by whispered spells,
He wore a mask, a heavy guise,
In search of love, beneath the lies.

Each step he took on fractured ground,
A lonely echo, no solace found,
For every smile, a hidden scar,
A longing soul, a distant star.

He danced with doubt, embraced the pain,
In crowded rooms, he felt the strain,
A yearning cry, a silent plea,
To be seen whole, to simply be.

But walls were built, and doors were closed,
In every glance, rejection posed,
Yet hope, a flicker, refused to die,
A fragile dream beneath the sky.

Then came the light, a gentle spark,
The PEC team, igniting the dark,
With open arms, they broke the chains,
In laughter shared, he shed his pains.

No longer lost, he found his place,
In every heart, a warm embrace,
For here, acceptance bloomed like spring,
A symphony of belonging.

Now tears of joy, like rivers flow,
For in their love, he's free to grow,
A tapestry of souls entwined,
At last, he's home, at last, he's kind.

In every heartbeat, every sigh,
He learned to soar, to touch the sky,
For in their eyes, he saw the truth,
That being himself was his greatest proof.

From Ashes to Wings

In the depths where shadows linger,
Where hope was but a whisper,
I wandered through the corridors of despair,
Each step a weight, each breath a prayer.

Life, a tempest, fierce and wild,
Stripped me bare, a broken child,
With every blow, the darkness crept,
In silence, I wept, in silence, I wept.

The flames of anguish danced around,
A hellish symphony, a haunting sound,
I wore my scars like chains of lead,
A tapestry of sorrow, a heart misled.

Yet in that void, a flicker glowed,
A spark of strength, a seed bestowed,
From ashes cold, a whisper grew,
"Rise, oh spirit, rise anew."

With trembling hands, I grasped the light,
A flicker turned to a blazing fight,
I shed the skin of pain and fear,
Embraced the truth that I was here.

The phoenix stirs in the heart of night,
With wings of fire, it takes to flight,
From the ruins of anguish, I emerged whole,
A testament of spirit, a reborn soul.

Each tear I shed, a river wide,
Carried the weight of the pain inside,
But in that current, I found my way,
A path of healing, a brand new day.

Now I stand, a warrior bold,
With stories of battles, with tales untold,
For every scar, a lesson learned,
In the furnace of life, my spirit burned.

So let the world see my radiant glow,
A heart once shattered, now a vibrant show,
From the ashes of hell, I rise and sing,
A symphony of hope, on phoenix wings.

And if you find yourself in despair,
Know that the darkness cannot compare,
To the light that waits, just beyond the fight,
For in every ending, there's a chance for flight.

So weep for the past, but do not stay,
For the dawn will break, and lead the way,
From the depths of sorrow, we shall ascend,
With hearts intertwined, we rise, we mend.

Fractured Chains

In the silence of the night, I hear the whispers call,
A siren song of shadows, where I once would fall.
The needle's cold embrace, a fleeting, false delight,
But in its grasp, I lost myself, consumed by endless night.

Each high a fleeting moment, a spark that fades away,
A dance with fleeting euphoria, a price I had to pay.
The laughter turned to echoes, the joy became a ghost,
In the depths of my addiction, I learned to fear the most.

I wore my pain like armour, a shield against the light,
But every time I stumbled, I lost another fight.
The faces of my loved ones, blurred through a haze of tears,
Their voices filled with worry, their hearts consumed by fears.

I chased the fleeting dragon, thought I could tame the flame,
But every time I caught it, it only brought me shame.
The promises I shattered, the trust I left behind,
In the wreckage of my choices, I searched but could not find.

Yet in the darkest moments, a flicker starts to glow,
A whisper of redemption, a path I long to know.
With trembling hands, I reach for hope, a lifeline in the storm,
To break these fractured chains, to find a new, true form.

Each step is filled with struggle, each day a brand new fight,
But I'm learning to embrace the dawn, to welcome in the light.
The road is long and winding, with scars that tell my tale,
But I'll rise from the ashes, I refuse to let me fail.

So here I stand, unsteady, but ready to reclaim,
The pieces of my shattered self, to rise above the shame.
With every breath, I'm healing, with every tear, I grow,
In the journey of recovery, I'm learning how to glow.

Though the past may haunt me, it won't define my way,
I'll forge a path of courage, I'll find a brighter day.
For in the heart of struggle, I've found a strength anew,
In the battle for my freedom, I'm learning to be true.

Shadows of Jack

(Verse 1)
In the quiet of the night, I hear your laughter fade,
A memory so vivid, now a ghost that won't escape.
We were two souls dancing, in a world that felt so right,
But the darkness came and stole you, left me lost in endless night.

(Pre-Chorus)
I still see your smile, it lights up my mind,
But the pain of your absence, it's a weight I can't unwind.
Every corner of this town, whispers your name,
And I'm left here shattered, drowning in the blame.

(Chorus)
Oh Jack, you were my heartbeat, my guiding star,
Now I'm lost in the shadows, wondering where you are.
The world feels so empty, without you by my side,
I'm a survivor of the silence, but I'm breaking inside.
You were my best friend, my soulmate, my light,
Now I'm fighting through the darkness, trying to find the fight.

(Verse 2)
I remember our dreams, the plans we made to soar,
But now I'm haunted by the echoes of what was before.
I wear your memory like a scar upon my heart,
A reminder of the love that was torn apart.

(Pre-Chorus)
I still hear your voice, it calls me from the past,
But the weight of this sorrow, it's a shadow that won't pass.
Every tear that falls, it's a piece of my soul,
And I'm left here searching for a way to feel whole.

(Chorus)
Oh Jack, you were my heartbeat, my guiding star,
Now I'm lost in the shadows, wondering where you are.
The world feels so empty, without you by my side,
I'm a survivor of the silence, but I'm breaking inside.
You were my best friend, my soulmate, my light,
Now I'm fighting through the darkness, trying to find the fight.

(Bridge)
I wish I could turn back time, hold you close once more,
Tell you that I love you, that you're worth fighting for.
But the night took you away, left me with this pain,
And I'm learning how to breathe, but it feels like I'm in chains.

(Chorus)
Oh Jack, you were my heartbeat, my guiding star,
Now I'm lost in the shadows, wondering where you are.
The world feels so empty, without you by my side,
I'm a survivor of the silence, but I'm breaking inside.
You were my best friend, my soulmate, my light,
Now I'm fighting through the darkness, trying to find the fight.

(Outro)
So I'll carry your spirit, in every tear I cry,
You'll forever be my angel, watching from the sky.
Though the pain may never fade, I'll learn to live again,
For you, my dear Jack, I'll find the strength within.
In the shadows, I'll remember, the love that we once shared,
And though you're gone, my soulmate, I know you always cared.

Echoes of Absence

In the shadows where demons danced,
I wandered lost, entranced by chance.
A siren's call, a whispering lie,
In the depths of despair, I learned to fly.

Chains of addiction wrapped tight around,
In the hell of my choices, I was bound.
Each hit, each drink, a fleeting escape,
But the price was my soul, a heart left to scrape.

I stumbled through nights, a ghost in the haze,
Chasing the high in a labyrinth of maze.
But the laughter turned hollow, the colours turned grey,
In the grip of the darkness, I lost my way.

Then a flicker of hope, a glimmer of light,
A voice in the silence, "You can still fight."
With trembling resolve, I stepped to the floor,
The gym became sanctuary, a path to restore.

Iron and sweat, the weights felt like chains,
But each lift, each push, released all my pains.
With every heartbeat, I shattered the mold,
From ashes of sorrow, a new story told.

The mirror reflected a warrior's face,
No longer a victim, I found my own grace.
Muscles grew stronger, but deeper within,
I forged a new spirit, a battle to win.

The echoes of struggle, they still linger near,
But I've learned to embrace them, to hold them dear.
For every scar tells a tale of the fight,
Of rising from darkness, of reclaiming the light.

Freedom is found in the rhythm of breath,
In the pulse of the gym, in the dance with death.
I've traded my demons for strength and for peace,
In the heart of the struggle, I found my release.

Now I stand tall, with the weight of my past,
A phoenix reborn, from the ashes I've cast.
With each drop of sweat, I honour the pain,
For in the embrace of the struggle, I've learned to remain.

So here's to the journey, the battles we face,
To the power of healing, the beauty of grace.
From hell to the heavens, I've forged my own way,
In the freedom of movement, I choose to stay.

From Ashes to Strength

In the quiet of the night, where shadows softly creep,
A mother's heart is heavy, in memories she weeps.
Two years of laughter stolen, like whispers in the breeze,
A baby boy named Zoran, now resting 'neath the trees.

I never held you, brother, never felt your tiny hand,
Yet in the depths of longing, I feel you understand.
Your laughter echoes softly, a melody so sweet,
In dreams, I see you dancing, your little heart's heartbeat.

Your cot stands still and empty, a shrine of what could be,
With clothes untouched, still folded, a testament to thee.
I picture you in sunlight, arms raised to the sky,
"Doviđenja" softly playing, as you twirl and fly.

Oh, how my mother mourns you, her baby boy, her light,
Each tear a silent story, each sigh a whispered night.
She cradles all the moments, the dreams that slipped away,
In every corner of her heart, you forever will stay.

I feel your spirit near me, in the rustle of the leaves,
In the laughter of the children, in the warmth of summer eves.
Though time may steal the present, and shadows may obscure,
The bond we share, dear Zoran, is a love that will endure.

So here I stand, a witness, to the love that never fades,
To the joy and to the sorrow, in the memories we've made.
Though I never met you, brother, your essence fills the air,
In the dance of life and longing, I know you're always there.

In the silence of your cot, where dreams and echoes blend,
I hold you close, dear Zoran, my brother, my lost friend.
And as the music lingers, in the twilight's gentle glow,
I'll carry you within me, wherever I may go.

Dear Family,

In the quiet hours when shadows creep,
I pen these words, my heart laid bare,
A letter forged in sorrow's keep,
A plea for love, a cry for care.

I wear a mask, a painted smile,
But underneath, the tempest roars,
Each day a battle, each night a trial,
A war within, behind closed doors.

These demons dance, they whisper low,
With promises sweet, they lure me near,
They wrap their chains, they steal my glow,
And drown my hope in pools of fear.

I see your faces, bright and kind,
Yet in my chest, a hollow ache,
I'm lost in fog, I'm blind, I'm blind,
A prisoner of the choices I make.

I want to fight, I want to flee,
To break these bonds, to find the light,
But every time I try to be,
They pull me back into the night.

I've seen your tears, I've felt your pain,
The weight of love, a heavy shroud,
I'm sorry for the hurt I've lain,
For every promise lost, unbowed.

I wish I could erase the scars,
The nights I've stolen, the trust I've burned,
But here I am, beneath the stars,
A soul that's broken, a heart that's turned.

I hear your voices, soft and clear,
"Come home, come home," you gently plead,
But in this darkness, I live in fear,
Of the monster that I've come to need.

I'm fighting hard, I swear I am,
But every step feels like a fall,
I'm caught in webs, a fragile sham,
A puppet to the siren's call.

So here I stand, on trembling ground,
A ghost of who I used to be,
I long for peace, for love profound,
But the chains are strong, they won't set me free.

If I could turn back time, I'd choose,
To hold you close, to never stray,
But here I am, with all I lose,
A heart that's heavy, a soul in grey.

Forgive me, please, for all I've done,
For every moment I've let you down,
I'm still your child, though I've come undone,
A weary traveller in this town.

I'll keep on fighting, I'll keep on trying,
For you, for me, for love's embrace,
But know this truth, as I'm sighing,
I'm lost in shadows, I'm lost in space.

So hold me close, don't let me go,
In this dark night, be my guiding star,
For in your love, I'll find the glow,
And maybe, just maybe, I'll heal the scar.

With all my love,
Your weary soul.

Echoes of a Shattered Dream

In the quiet of the night, when shadows creep,
A soul once vibrant, now lost in sleep,
With trembling hands and a heart so frail,
Chasing whispers of a ghostly trail.

Once a child with dreams that soared,
Now a prisoner, forever ignored,
Each promise made, a fragile thread,
Tangled in the lies that fill her head.

She dances with demons, a twisted waltz,
In the mirror's reflection, she sees her faults,
A smile painted on, but the eyes betray,
The war within that won't fade away.

The needle's kiss, a lover's embrace,
In the depths of despair, she finds her place,
A fleeting high, a moment's grace,
But the morning light reveals the trace.

Her mother's tears, like rain on stone,
A heart that aches, forever alone,
"Come back to me," the whispers plead,
But the chains of addiction plant their seed.

Friends turn to ghosts, their laughter fades,
In the haze of smoke, the memory wades,
Once a sister, a confidante, a friend,
Now a shadow, a means to an end.

The world spins on, indifferent, cold,
While she fights a battle, silent and bold,
Each hit a promise, each pill a lie,
In the depths of her soul, she longs to fly.

But the grip is tight, the darkness deep,
In the silence, she weeps, in the silence, she weeps,
For the life she lost, for the love she craved,
For the dreams that slipped through fingers enslaved.

So here's to the souls, lost in the night,
To the flickering candles, dimming their light,
May we hold them close, may we hear their cries,
For in their struggle, our humanity lies.

Let us break the chains, let us mend the seams,
For every lost heart still holds its dreams,
In the battle of shadows, let love be the spark,
To guide them back home from the whispers in the dark.

In the Silence of War

In the dawn's early light, we lace up our boots,
With hearts full of courage, and heavy with roots,
We march into shadows where nightmares reside,
With brothers beside us, our fears we confide.

The drums of the distant, a thunderous call,
We leave behind laughter, we leave behind all,
For duty and honour, we carry the weight,
Yet deep in our souls, we question our fate.

The sun beats down on the dust and the grime,
Each step a reminder of the passage of time,
The faces of strangers, now etched in my mind,
Their hopes and their dreams, in the chaos confined.

In the heart of the battle, the world turns to grey,
The cries of the fallen, they echo and sway,
I reach for a hand, but it slips through my grasp,
A moment of silence, a breath held, a gasp.

The laughter of children, now distant and faint,
Replaced by the thunder, the cries of the saint,
I carry their stories, their dreams and their fears,
In the silence of war, I drown in my tears.

The nights stretch like shadows, the memories creep,
In the stillness of darkness, I struggle to sleep,
The faces of comrades, their voices still near,
In the silence of war, I'm haunted by fear.

What is it to fight for a land that I love,
When the cost of that love is a push and a shove?
To stand for the fallen, to honour the brave,
Yet feel like a ghost in the life that I crave.

I wear my medals, but they weigh like a stone,
Each one a reminder of battles alone,
The laughter of home, now a whispering ghost,
In the silence of war, I long for it most.

I write to my loved ones, my heart on the page,
But the words feel so hollow, like a bird in a cage,
I tell them I'm fine, that I'm strong and I'll cope,
Yet inside I'm unravelling, searching for hope.

For every life saved, a piece of me dies,
In the echoes of gunfire, in the last desperate cries,
I carry their burdens, their hopes and their dreams,
In the silence of war, nothing's as it seems.

So when you see soldiers, know we bear the scars,
Of battles unspoken, of invisible wars,
For in the silence of war, we fight to be free,
Yet the torment within is a part of our plea.

In the dawn's early light, we lace up our boots,
With hearts full of courage, and heavy with roots,
We march on together, through shadows and pain,
For the love of our country, we'll rise up again.

In the Heart of the Storm

In the quiet before the tempest roars,
We gather, hearts heavy, at the open doors,
With boots laced tight and courage worn thin,
We stand as one, ready to begin.

The sirens wail, a haunting call,
A cry for help, a plea from the fall,
We rush to the chaos, to the shattered ground,
Where hope is lost, and fear is found.

With every step, the weight of despair,
The faces of strangers, the burden we share,
In the eyes of the lost, I see my own pain,
A mirror reflecting the heart's silent strain.

We dig through the rubble, we sift through the ash,
Each moment a memory, each heartbeat a clash,
Of laughter and love, of lives intertwined,
Yet here in the wreckage, what solace can find?

I hold a child, her teddy bear torn,
A mother's soft whisper, "Please, keep her warm,"
But in my chest, a tempest brews,
For every life saved, another one loses.

The nights stretch long, the shadows creep,
In the silence that follows, I struggle to sleep,
The faces of those I couldn't save,
Haunt my dreams like a restless wave.

I wear a brave smile, a shield of resolve,
But inside, the questions begin to dissolve,
Did I do enough? Could I have tried more?
The echoes of doubt, a relentless roar.

In the heart of the storm, I find my place,
Yet in every rescue, I feel the embrace,
Of grief and of joy, of loss and of gain,
A tapestry woven with threads of pain.

I am the hand that reaches through night,
The voice that whispers, "You'll be alright,"
But who holds the heart of the one who gives?
In the silence, I wonder, how long will I live?

For every life touched, a piece of me stays,
In the stories of courage, in the darkest of days,
I carry their burdens, their hopes and their fears,
A volunteer's heart, soaked in silent tears.

So when you see us, know we are there,
With love in our hearts, and a weight we bear,
For in every rescue, in every embrace,
We are the echoes of a world's broken grace.

And as the storms rage and the skies turn grey,
We stand together, come what may,
For in the heart of the storm, we find our way,
A family of souls, in the light of the fray.

Resilient Heart

In the shadows where whispers dwell,
I've fed the mouths that cursed my name,
With every bite, a silent spell,
A dance of love wrapped in their shame.

I've wiped the tears from faces cold,
Those who've carved my heart with knives,
Yet still, I gather strength untold,
In the wreckage, my spirit thrives.

I've lifted souls from depths of night,
Those who sought to drag me down,
With every hand I've reached in fight,
I wore their burdens like a crown.

I've done the favours, given grace,
To those who'd turn and walk away,
In kindness, I've found my own embrace,
A light that guides me through the fray.

Crazy? Maybe, but here I stand,
A warrior forged in love and pain,
With scars that map this weary land,
I rise again, I break the chain.

I will not lose myself in spite,
Nor drown in hatred's bitter sea,
For in the dark, I find my light,
I am who I am, unapologetically.

Life isn't easy, it's a storm,
Yet through the chaos, I remain,
With every bruise, I've been reborn,
In every tear, I've found my flame.

So let them talk, let them conspire,
Their demons dance, but I won't bend,
For in my heart, a fierce desire,
To love, to heal, to never end.

I'll stand my ground, I'll face the fight,
With every breath, I claim my right,
To be the truth, to be the free,
To live my life, unapologetically me.

Behind the Mask

In the quiet corners of a crowded room,
Where laughter dances, and shadows loom,
He wears a smile, a crafted guise,
But deep within, the tempest lies.

With shoulders broad, he carries the weight,
Of unspoken battles, of a silent fate.
"Be strong," they say, "don't show your tears,"
Yet inside, he's drowning in unvoiced fears.

The world demands a warrior's heart,
But who will mend the broken parts?
He fights the demons that whisper and sneer,
"Real men don't cry; they swallow their fear."

Each morning he wakes, a soldier in strife,
With scars that are hidden, a fractured life.
He walks through the day, a ghost in the light,
While shadows of doubt consume him at night.

In the mirror, he sees a stranger's face,
A mask of bravado, a hollow embrace.
The laughter of friends feels distant, surreal,
As he battles the darkness, the pain that won't heal.

He's told to be tough, to toughen his skin,
But the weight of the world is a burden within.
With every "man up," a piece of him dies,
As he fights for his worth beneath judgmental eyes.

The phone stays silent, no calls to confide,
In a world that demands he should swallow his pride.
He yearns for connection, for someone to see,
The man behind the mask, the soul that's not free.

But stigma is heavy, a chain made of shame,
And he fears that his truth will be met with disdain.
So he bottles his anguish, his sorrow, his plight,
While the demons keep dancing, consuming the light.

He dreams of a day when the walls will come down,
When vulnerability wears a compassionate crown.
When men can be tender, and hearts can be bare,
When the strength of a tear is a badge that we wear.

So listen, dear world, to the cries that you miss,
To the men who are fighting for solace, for bliss.
Let's shatter the silence, let's break through the mold,
For the bravest of hearts are the ones that are told:

"It's okay to feel, it's okay to break,
To reach for a hand, to admit when you ache.
You're not alone in this battle you face,
Together we'll rise, together we'll grace."

So let the tears flow, let the truth be unfurled,
For the strength of a man is his heart in this world.
And in every drop, let compassion ignite,
For the demons we battle can't dim our light.

In Shadows We Dwell

In the quiet corners of a crowded room,
Where laughter dances, and joy finds bloom,
I wear a mask, a fragile disguise,
But beneath the surface, my spirit cries.

A tempest brews in my restless mind,
A war of shadows, where hope's hard to find.
I'm painted with colours, vibrant yet stark,
A canvas of chaos, a flickering spark.

They see the bravado, the strength I portray,
But inside, I'm crumbling, I'm fading away.
"Just be a man," they say with disdain,
But they don't know the weight of this invisible chain.

I reach for connection, for hands that can hold,
But stigma wraps tighter, a grip icy cold.
"Why can't you just think? Why can't you just feel?"
As if my existence is something unreal.

I'm haunted by demons, they whisper my name,
In the silence of night, they stoke the same flame.
"Unworthy, unlovable, lost in the fray,"
They echo my fears, they lead me astray.

I've battled the darkness, I've fought through the pain,
But the scars on my heart are a heavy chain.
I've lost friends to silence, to judgment, to scorn,
In a world that's unkind, I feel so forlorn.

I scream for support, but the echoes fall flat,
In a society blind, where compassion is spat.
"Just toughen up, soldier, don't show your despair,"
But the weight of my sorrow is too much to bear.

I've watched as the light in my brothers has dimmed,
As they wrestle with shadows, their spirits untrimmed.
Some find their release in the depths of the night,
In the silence of darkness, they slip from the fight.

Oh, the stories untold, the lives left behind,
The men who were warriors, yet never defined.
By the strength of their hearts, or the battles they've fought,
But by whispers of weakness, by the stigma they've caught.

So here I stand, with my heart on my sleeve,
A plea for compassion, a chance to believe.
That we're more than our struggles, more than our scars,
That we're worthy of love, no matter how far.

Let's shatter the silence, let's break down the walls,
For the men who are fighting, who hear the dark calls.
Let's lift up our voices, let's stand side by side,
In a world that is kinder, where no one must hide.

For in the depths of despair, there's a flicker of light,
A hope that can flourish, a reason to fight.
So let's hold each other, let's banish the shame,
For together we rise, and we'll never be the same.

Fragmented Echoes

In the hollow chambers of my mind,
Where shadows dance and whispers bind,
A fractured self, a ghostly wraith,
I wander lost, devoid of faith.

The mirror shatters, shards of me,
Reflections of a soul set free,
Yet bound in chains of silent screams,
I drift through half-remembered dreams.

Demons lurk in corners dark,
With eyes like embers, cold and stark,
They pull me down to depths unknown,
Where every heartbeat feels alone.

I wear a mask, a painted guise,
To hide the storm behind my eyes,
But in the quiet, when night descends,
The weight of silence never ends.

I reach for hands that slip away,
Like grains of sand at break of day,
Each touch a memory, faint and frail,
A shipwrecked heart, a ghostly sail.

The laughter echoes, distant, thin,
A haunting tune where I've been,
Yet here I stand, a hollow shell,
A prisoner in my own farewell.

The world spins on, a vibrant hue,
While I am lost, a shade of blue,
Each moment stretches, time stands still,
A void that swallows, a bitter chill.

I scream for help, but words betray,
They twist and turn, then fade away,
In crowded rooms, I'm all alone,
A silent cry, a heart of stone.

Yet in this darkness, a flicker glows,
A fragile spark that gently grows,
For even in the depths of night,
A whisper stirs, a hint of light.

So I will gather every shard,
And piece together what's been marred,
With trembling hands, I'll forge anew,
A tapestry of me, of you.

For though the demons claw and bite,
I'll rise again, reclaim my light,
In every tear, a story told,
In every scar, a heart of gold.

And when the echoes fade away,
I'll find my voice, I'll learn to stay,
For in the chaos, I will see,
The strength to be, the strength in me.

The Weight of Choices

In the quiet of a restless night,
When shadows stretch and whispers bite,
You stand at the edge of a precipice,
A heart heavy with the weight of choice,
The echo of a voice that trembles,
"Will you leap, or will you stay?"

If you hadn't made that one hard decision,
The world would have remained a muted hue,
A canvas untouched, a song unsung,
And you would have never known
The taste of fear that ignites the soul,
The fire that burns through the veil of comfort.

You wouldn't have faced the storms,
The relentless waves that crashed upon your shore,
Each one a challenge, a shattering blow,
That broke you into pieces,
Like glass scattered on the floor,
Sharp and glimmering, a painful beauty.

But in the wreckage, you found the light,
A flicker of strength, a whisper of hope,
That rose from the ashes,
Like a phoenix, fierce and unyielding,
Rebuilding the ruins of your heart,
Brick by fragile brick.

You wouldn't have met the souls
Who danced in the dark with you,
Who held your hand through the chaos,
Who painted your world with colours
You never knew existed,
Each one a brush stroke of love,
Each one a lesson in the art of living.

And oh, the path you walked,
Twisted and tangled,
Felt like a cruel joke at times,
But it was the road that led you home,
To the place where dreams unfurl,
Where the heart finds its rhythm,
Where the soul sings its truth.

Sometimes, it's the moments we dread,
The ones we wish to erase,
That carve the deepest lines in our story,
Etching the beauty of resilience,
The grace of survival,
The bittersweet taste of becoming.

The hardest detours,
Those jagged turns of fate,
They lead us to the most beautiful destinations,
Where the sun breaks through the clouds,
And the heart, once shattered,
Beats with a fierce, unrelenting love.

So let the tears fall, let them flow,
For they are the rain that nourishes the earth,
The proof of a journey,
The testament of a life lived fully,
Where every choice, every leap,
Is a thread woven into the tapestry of you.

And in the end, when the night is still,
And the stars whisper secrets of the brave,
You'll know that every hard decision,
Every moment of doubt,
Was a step toward the life you dreamed,
A life that was waiting,
Just waiting,
For you to take that leap.

In the Beautiful Mess

Happiness isn't a polished gem,
Not a map with every road defined,
It's the laughter in the chaos,
The dance of the heart, unconfined.

In the tangled threads of our days,
Where shadows stretch and doubts collide,
We stumble through the wild maze,
Yet in our hearts, the light won't hide.

Oh, how we grasp at fleeting dreams,
With hands that tremble, hearts that ache,
We wear our scars like silver seams,
Each tear a river, each breath a quake.

We laugh at the mistakes we make,
As if the world could hear our song,
In every fall, a chance to wake,
In every right, a place for wrong.

So let the chaos swirl around,
Let the storms rage, let the thunder roll,
For in the mess, our truths are found,
In every crack, the light can stroll.

And when the night feels cold and long,
When silence wraps its heavy shroud,
Remember, love, you still belong,
Your heart knows joy, though the mind feels cowed.

Dance with your chaos, embrace the fight,
For every stumble, a step to grace,
In the beautiful mess, we find our light,
In the tangled journey, we find our place.

So let the tears fall, let the laughter rise,
In the symphony of life, we play our part,
For happiness blooms in the darkest skies,
And joy is the echo of a brave, beating heart.

In the end, it's not about the perfect score,
But the courage to dance, to love, to feel,
To find joy in the mess, to open the door,
To a life that's imperfect, yet beautifully real.

The Legacy of a Big Kid

In a world that scoffs, where laughter cuts deep,
You stand, a big kid, with dreams that won't sleep.
With a heart like a canvas, painted wild and free,
You dance through the chaos, a child still in glee.

Oh, how they chuckle, those shadows of doubt,
When your inner child whispers, "Let's figure this out!"
But you cradle that spirit, that curious spark,
In the depths of your laughter, you light up the dark.

Life's rules are mere whispers, you test and you bend,
With reckless abandon, you refuse to pretend.
Each moment a treasure, each heartbeat a song,
In the symphony of living, you've always belonged.

You dream of the end, drifting sideways on fate,
A bike made of memories, a life that's first-rate.
Screaming, "Now THAT'S how you live!" as you glide,
With a grin on your face, and your heart open wide.

When the reel of your life plays its bittersweet tune,
You'll smile through the laughter, you'll weep with the moon.
For the love that you've woven, the joy that you've sown,
Will echo in hearts, in the seeds you have grown.

You've carved out a legacy, vibrant and bold,
A tapestry woven with stories retold.
In the laughter of children, in the warmth of a friend,
Your spirit will linger, your love will transcend.

So live, oh dear dreamer, with all of your might,
For we die only once, but we live in the light.
Leave behind what is treasured, what can't be erased,
A legacy glowing, a life fully embraced.

And when the last breath whispers, when shadows draw near,
Know you've danced through the chaos, with nothing to fear.
For the big kid inside you, forever will soar,
In the hearts of the loved ones, you've touched evermore.

Resurrection of the Silent

In the depths of despair, where shadows conspire,
I stood on the edge, consumed by the fire.
A whisper of darkness, a scream in my soul,
I felt like a puppet, no longer in control.

Once, I made the decision, a final decree,
To slip through the silence, to set my heart free.
No words could have reached me, no love could have swayed,
In that fleeting moment, my spirit decayed.

It was a battle within, a war I had fought,
But the mind turned to ashes, and hope came to naught.
I was just a vessel, a shell lost at sea,
With a heart that was heavy, and a soul that would flee.

Then came the stillness, the sweet, dark embrace,
As I whispered goodbye to this cold, cruel place.
My heart stopped its beating, my breath turned to mist,
In the silence, I lingered, in the void, I was kissed.

But life had a plan, a twist unforeseen,
In the chaos of darkness, a flicker of green.
Brought back to the surface, on a gurney I lay,
With the sheet almost ready to carry me away.

A friend, a fierce angel, with courage ablaze,
Stole the defibrillator, igniting my days.
She zapped me with hope, with a spark of the light,
And I gasped back to life, from the depths of the night.

The first jolt was futile, a whisper of fate,
But the second, it thundered, it shattered the weight.
In that moment of chaos, I felt the rebirth,
A reminder that life, despite all, has worth.

Yet the seconds were fleeting, a blink in the dark,
From "I'm done" to the void, a swift, silent arc.
So for those who are watching, who wish they had known,
You couldn't have saved me; I was lost in my own.

But here I stand now, a survivor reborn,
With scars that tell stories, with a heart that's been torn.
I carry the weight of the battles I've fought,
And the love that surrounds me, the lessons I've sought.

So let this be a beacon, a light in the night,
For those who are struggling, who've lost all their fight.
You are not alone; there's a hand that will reach,
In the depths of despair, there's a lesson to teach.

For life is a tapestry, woven with pain,
But in every dark moment, there's beauty to gain.
So hold on, dear warrior, through the storm and the strife,
For the echoes of silence can lead to new life.

And if you feel broken, if you feel like you're done,
Remember, there's hope, and you're not the only one.
In the depths of the shadows, let love be your guide,
For the heart that once faltered can learn how to rise.

Whispers of the Unbound

In the shadows where silence dwells,
Pain festers, a secret kept,
A weight that bends the strongest backs,
A wound that never wept.
Behind the bars of shame we hide,
Our hearts, a prison, cold and stark,
Each unspoken word, a heavy chain,
Each buried truth, a lingering dark.

We are only as sick as the hate we hold,
As the shame that clings like a second skin,
The silence suffocates, a thief in the night,
Stealing the light that dares to begin.
But listen – can you hear the whispers rise?
The echoes of souls, longing to be free,
They call from the depths, from the corners of pain,
"Speak us into existence, let us be."

For the moment we dare to break the seal,
To surrender our burdens to the air,
The chains that once bound us begin to dissolve,
The weight of our wounds, no longer a snare.
This is where healing ignites like a flame,
Not in the shadows, but in the embrace,
Of truth laid bare, of hearts unafraid,
In the light of connection, we find our place.

A healed heart does not merely beat,
It radiates warmth, it pulses with grace,
In alignment with whispers of souls intertwined,
No longer imprisoned by fear's cold embrace.
And love? Oh, love is a tempest, a storm,
Not just gentle, but fierce in its might,
It unravels the tightly wound threads of despair,
Transforms the darkness, ignites the night.

When we heal, we do not walk alone,
We become the catalysts, the sparks in the dark,
Touching the lives of those who are lost,
Creating ripples, igniting the spark.
We rise, we rise, together as one,
In a world where healing is no longer a dream,
Where love is our power, our anthem, our song,
Where we shatter the silence, let our voices scream.

So speak, release, let the truth take flight,
Let the burdens of yesterday fall to the ground,
For in the act of revealing our deepest despair,
We find the strength in the love that surrounds.
This is the shift, this is the revolution,
A world where we rise, where we heal, where we shine,
Together, unbound, in the light of our truth,
In the power of love, we are finally divine.

When Bad Things End

In the quiet of the night, when shadows creep,
Two hearts once entwined, now secrets they keep.
Sometimes you're good, but together, you're bad,
A love that once flourished, now leaves you both sad.

Mums and dads don't last forever, they say,
Yet in the echoes of laughter, they slowly decay.
Promises whispered in the soft morning light,
Now linger like ghosts in the depths of the night.

Gotta end the chapter to read the next,
A story unwritten, a life unvexed.
Not the best husband, but a better ex,
In the wreckage of love, we find what comes next.

Sometimes marriage falls apart at the seams,
A tapestry frayed, unravelling dreams.
To break and to make two stronger hearts,
Is to learn that from endings, a new journey starts.

Can't call her wife, guess you'll have to call friend,
In the ashes of love, new beginnings can mend.
Good things start when bad things end,
But oh, the weight of the love that we spend.

The laughter that echoed, the tears that we shed,
The moments we cherished, now hang by a thread.
In the silence that follows, the heartache remains,
A bittersweet symphony, a dance of the pains.

So here's to the memories, both bitter and sweet,
To the love that we lost, to the paths that we meet.
For sometimes you're good, but together, you're not,
And in letting go, we find what we sought.

So let the tears flow, let the heartache be known,
For in every ending, a new seed is sown.
And though it may hurt, as we learn to transcend,
Remember, dear heart, good things start when bad things end.

The Keeper of Secrets

In English, they say: "Best friend,"
But in poetry, we weave a thread,
A tapestry of laughter and tears,
A bond that whispers through the years.

The keeper of secrets, the healer of pain,
A heart that dances in sunshine and rain,
With every shared moment, a promise is made,
In the shadows of sorrow, our memories cascade.

We carved our names in the bark of old trees,
Spoke dreams to the stars, felt the soft summer breeze,
In the warmth of your laughter, I found my own light,
But shadows grew longer, and day turned to night.

You held my hand through the storms of despair,
With a gaze that said, "I will always be there."
But time, that thief, with its cruel, silent tread,
Stole moments away, left whispers instead.

Now I stand in the echoes of what used to be,
A ghost of your laughter, a fading decree,
The keeper of secrets, now lost in the fray,
A bond unbroken, yet drifting away.

I remember the promises, the dreams we once spun,
The battles we fought, the victories won,
But life is a river, relentless and wide,
And I'm left here alone, with the tide as my guide.

Your chair sits empty, your voice a soft sigh,
The world feels so heavy, the days passing by,
I search for your shadow in every bright dawn,
But the keeper of secrets is forever gone.

In the silence, I hear all the words left unsaid,
The laughter that lingered, the tears that we shed,
And though I am broken, I'll carry your name,
For love is eternal, and loss is the same.

So here's to the moments, the joy and the pain,
To the keeper of secrets, who danced in the rain,
Though the bond may be severed, the love will remain,
In the heart of the poet, where memories reign.

In the Depths of Shadows

Once, I danced on sunlit shores,
Where laughter echoed, and hope soared,
Each heartbeat a promise, each breath a song,
In the arms of joy, I felt I belonged.

But the tides turned, as they often do,
And the sky, once bright, turned a sorrowful hue.
The weight of the world, a familiar embrace,
Pulled me back down to that desolate place.

I fought through the darkness, clawed at the light,
With every small victory, I felt I could fight.
But the shadows are patient, they whisper and creep,
And one fateful morning, they stole all my sleep.

Now I sit in the silence, a storm in my chest,
With thoughts that are heavy, a heart that won't rest.
The laughter has faded, the colours have bled,
And I'm left with the echoes of words left unsaid.

I think of my daughter, her smile like the dawn,
A light in my life, a reason to carry on.
Yet here in this darkness, I'm lost and alone,
With a heart full of sorrow, a mind turned to stone.

I draft an email, my fingers tremble slow,
"Make sure she knows, I loved her so."
But the words feel like chains, binding me tight,
As I teeter on edges, consumed by the night.

Where is the way out? I search for a sign,
But the path is obscured, the stars refuse to shine.
I'm drowning in silence, in thoughts that confound,
In a world that feels heavy, where hope can't be found.

Oh, to feel awesome, to bask in the glow,
To rise from the ashes, to let the heart grow.
But the depths of despair are a cruel, bitter friend,
And I'm weary of fighting, I'm tired of pretend.

So I sit with my sorrow, a ghost in the dark,
With a heart full of love, yet a soul that feels stark.
If you read this, dear friend, know I tried to hold on,
But the shadows are fierce, and I fear I am gone.

In the depths of this struggle, I wish you could see,
The beauty in life, the light that could be.
But if I must leave, let my love be the guide,
For in every heartbeat, I'll be by your side.

So remember the laughter, the joy that we shared,
And know that I fought, that I truly cared.
In the depths of this darkness, I hope you will find,
The strength to keep going, the love left behind.

In the Quiet of Shadows

In our darkest moments, when the world feels cold,
We don't seek solutions, nor wisdom retold.
What we yearn for is simple, a touch soft and near,
A presence that whispers, "You're safe, I am here."

Please don't try to fix me, don't bear my despair,
Don't push away shadows that linger in air.
Just sit by my side as I weather the storm,
Be the steady hand that keeps my heart warm.

My pain is a burden, a weight I must bear,
These battles are mine, fought in silence and care.
Yet your quiet reminder, your love in the night,
Tells me I'm worthy, even when I lose sight.

In the vastness of darkness, where fears intertwine,
Your presence, a beacon, a lifeline divine.
When I falter and tremble, when hope feels so far,
You're the light that ignites the forgotten star.

So in those bleak hours, when I lose my way,
Will you just be here, not a saviour, but stay?
Hold my hand gently, as the dawn starts to break,
Help me remember the strength I can take.

Your silent support is a treasure untold,
A love that reminds me, even when I feel cold.
In the depths of my sorrow, when I'm lost in the fray,
You're the whisper of courage that guides me each day.

So let us sit quietly, in the stillness of night,
As I navigate shadows, you'll be my soft light.
For in this connection, this bond that we share,
I find the strength to rise, knowing you truly care.

And when the dawn breaks, with its golden embrace,
I'll carry your love, a warm, sacred space.
For in the quiet of shadows, I've learned to believe,
That even in darkness, it's love that we weave.

Whispers of the Silent Storm

In the stillness of night, where shadows creep,
A tempest brews quietly, where no one can peep.
Inside this fragile heart, a war rages on,
A battlefield of silence, where hope feels withdrawn.

I wear a mask of calm, a smile painted bright,
But beneath the surface, I'm lost in the fight.
The demons are whispering, their voices so sly,
"Who will love you, dear one, when you're broken inside?"

Each day is a dance on a razor's thin edge,
A tightrope of feelings, a perilous pledge.
I long for connection, yet fear it will shatter,
The weight of my longing, a heart that feels battered.

I'm haunted by echoes of love that once bloomed,
Yet shadows of doubt in my mind are entombed.
"Am I worthy of kindness? Am I worthy of grace?"
These questions, like daggers, carve lines on my face.

I feel everything deeply, like waves crashing down,
A flood of emotions, a crown made of frown.
Joy turns to sorrow, like night turns to day,
In the blink of an eye, my heart's led astray.

I battle the silence, the screams in my chest,
The longing for solace, the need for a rest.
But the world keeps on spinning, oblivious, blind,
To the chaos that rages, the storms in my mind.

I'm a ghost in the daylight, a shadow at dusk,
A whisper of laughter, a heart turned to rust.
I crave understanding, a hand that won't shake,
But fear that my truth is too heavy to take.

So I sit in the quiet, where no one can see,
The hell that I carry, the weight of the sea.
And though I am silent, my heart's full of screams,
A tapestry woven with frayed, broken dreams.

If you could just glimpse through the veil of my soul,
You'd see the raw edges, the pieces not whole.
You'd feel the deep longing, the ache of the night,
The battle for peace, the relentless fight.

But in this dark journey, I search for a spark,
A flicker of kindness to light up the dark.
For even in chaos, there's beauty to find,
A thread of connection that binds heart to mind.

So if you should meet me, in silence or storm,
Know that I'm fighting, just trying to warm.
To find in the shadows a glimmer of grace,
A place where my heart can feel safe in its space.

And though I may tremble, and though I may break,
I'm learning to rise, for my own heart's sake.
In the whispers of silence, I'll find my own song,
For even in darkness, I know I belong.

Echoes of Emptiness

In the mirror's reflection, a stranger stares back,
A hollowed-out vessel, a heart under attack.
I wear a façade, a mask made of glass,
But inside, I'm a desert, where no rivers pass.

The world spins around me, vibrant and bright,
Yet I'm lost in the shadows, consumed by the night.
I reach for the colours, the laughter, the light,
But my fingers slip through, like dreams in the flight.

I'm a ghost in the crowd, a whisper unheard,
A symphony silent, a song without words.
The laughter of others, a distant refrain,
While I'm trapped in a silence, a prison of pain.

What is this numbness that clings to my skin?
A fog that envelops, a battle within.
I scream in the silence, but no one can hear,
The echoes of anguish, the weight of my fear.

I crave the connection, the warmth of a hand,
But the closer I reach, the more I can't stand.
For love feels like fire, yet I'm frozen in place,
A paradox tangled, a heart's cruel embrace.

I'm haunted by shadows, by whispers of doubt,
"Will they see the real me? Will they figure me out?"
I'm a puzzle unmade, with pieces that hide,
A tempest of feelings, a storm deep inside.

The demons are patient, they linger and leer,
They feed on my silence, they thrive on my fear.
"Unworthy, unlovable," they chant in my mind,
A chorus of anguish, a truth so unkind.

I wander through moments, a specter of time,
Each heartbeat a question, each breath a crime.
I'm lost in the echoes of what I can't say,
A prisoner of feelings that won't fade away.

And when the night falls, the darkness descends,
I'm left with the whispers, the thoughts that won't end.
I search for a meaning, a reason to fight,
But the emptiness swallows, devours the light.

I long for a language to speak what I feel,
To unravel the chaos, to make it all real.
But the words slip away, like sand through my hands,
And I'm left with the silence, the weight of demands.

So here I stand, trembling, a heart full of ache,
A soul that is weary, a spirit that breaks.
Yet in this vast emptiness, a flicker remains,
A hope that one day, I'll break free from these chains.

For even in darkness, there's a glimmer of grace,
A whisper of courage, a soft, warm embrace.
And though I may falter, and though I may fall,
I'll rise from the ashes, I'll answer the call.

So if you should see me, lost in the fray,
Know that I'm fighting, I'm searching for day.
For beneath all the numbness, the shadows, the pain,
There's a heart that is yearning, a soul to reclaim.

Ephemeral Echoes

In the quiet chambers of my mind,
Where shadows dance and whispers bind,
A fleeting warmth, a tender touch,
Yet in solitude, it fades to dust.

I gather love like autumn leaves,
Each vibrant hue, a heart that believes,
But when the sun dips low and dies,
I'm left with ghosts and hollow sighs.

Oh, the cruel trick of memory's game,
To hold me close, then leave me lame,
A symphony of laughter, now a distant hum,
In the silence, I'm lost, and I come undone.

I walk through gardens of past embrace,
Where smiles bloom, and time finds grace,
Yet as the twilight swallows the day,
I'm haunted by the love that slipped away.

Each friend, a star in my night sky bright,
But alone, I'm adrift, a ship without light,
The warmth of their words, a fleeting spark,
In the void of my heart, it's cold and dark.

I crave the permanence of a love that stays,
Yet I'm trapped in a cycle of ephemeral days,
The laughter, the kindness, all feel like a dream,
A mirage in the desert, a cruel, broken beam.

I reach for the echoes, but they slip through my hands,
Like grains of sand in forgotten lands,
And when the world fades, and I'm left to roam,
I wonder if love was ever my home.

So here I stand, a ghost of my own,
In a world full of faces, yet utterly alone,
The demons whisper, "You were never enough,"
And I drown in the silence, in the depths of my stuff.

But still, I'll gather the pieces, though they scatter and break,
For in the shards of my heart, there's a chance I can wake,
To find that the love, though fleeting and rare,
Is a flicker of hope in the depths of despair.

And maybe one day, when the shadows recede,
I'll learn to believe in the love that I need,
For though I may falter, and though I may fall,
I'll rise from the ashes, and I'll answer the call.

In the tapestry woven of joy and of pain,
I'll find my own thread, and I'll dance in the rain,
For even in darkness, a flicker can gleam,
And I'll hold onto love, as I chase down the dream.

Hollow Echoes

In the cavern of my chest, a void resides,
A chasm deep where hope collides,
With shadows that whisper, "You are not whole,"
A relentless ache that devours my soul.

I wear a mask, a painted guise,
To hide the emptiness behind my eyes,
But beneath the surface, a tempest brews,
A storm of emotions I cannot choose.

I scream for love in a silent night,
A desperate plea for a flicker of light,
Yet the echoes return, a haunting refrain,
"Why can't you feel? Why can't you contain?"

I rage like a wildfire, I weep like the rain,
Each outburst a cry, a release of the pain,
But the world looks on, with judgment and scorn,
And I'm left feeling broken, abandoned, and worn.

Oh, the demons that dance in the corners of my mind,
They taunt and they tease, they're cruel and unkind,
"Look at you, empty, a shell of a being,
A puppet of chaos, forever unseeing."

I reach for connection, but grasp at the air,
Each touch feels like glass, each glance a cold stare,
And when I am lost in the depths of despair,
I wonder if anyone truly could care.

The drama unfolds like a tragic play,
A desperate act to keep the abyss at bay,
But the more that I struggle, the more I retreat,
Into a world where the shadows and silence compete.

"Help me," I cry, but the words fall like stones,
In a sea of indifference, I drown all alone,
And the laughter of others feels distant and far,
As I search for a glimmer, a flicker, a star.

Yet in this abyss, a flicker remains,
A whisper of hope that softens the chains,
For though I am hollow, I still yearn to feel,
To break through the darkness, to find what is real.

So I'll gather the fragments, the shards of my heart,
And weave them together, though they're torn apart,
For even in emptiness, there's beauty to find,
A testament to strength, a spark of the mind.

And maybe one day, when the shadows recede,
I'll learn to embrace all the parts of me,
For though I may falter, and though I may break,
I'll rise from the ashes, and I'll learn to awake.

In the tapestry woven of sorrow and grace,
I'll find my own rhythm, my own sacred space,
For even in darkness, a flicker can gleam,
And I'll hold onto love, as I chase down the dream.

Whispers of the Abyss

In the mirror, a stranger stares back at me,
A fractured reflection, a soul lost at sea,
They call it a disorder, a label to wear,
But it's not a flaw; it's a burden I bear.

Emotional dysregulation, a tempest inside,
Feelings like waves, crashing, they collide,
One moment I'm soaring, the next I'm in chains,
A whirlwind of chaos, a dance with my pains.

I reach for the light, but it flickers and fades,
Each heartbeat a battle, each breath a charade,
The demons are whispering, "You're never enough,"
In a world full of colours, I'm lost in the rough.

I spiral like autumn leaves caught in the breeze,
A kaleidoscope of heartache, a heart that won't ease,
The laughter of others feels distant, a dream,
While I drown in the silence, a muted scream.

I grasp at the edges, the frayed threads of hope,
But the fabric unravels, I struggle to cope,
Impulsive decisions, a desperate embrace,
Of fleeting distractions that leave not a trace.

Oh, the hollowness echoes, a cavernous void,
A longing for solace, a heart that's destroyed,
I wear my emotions like armour, yet bare,
Each crack in my spirit, a testament to care.

They say I'm unstable, a tempest untamed,
But they don't see the battles, the scars that I've claimed,
For beneath the chaos, a flicker remains,
A whisper of strength that defies all the chains.

I'm not just a label, a shadow in flight,
I'm a tapestry woven of darkness and light,
And though I may falter, I'll rise from the fall,
For within this abyss, I am still standing tall.

So I'll gather the pieces, the shards of my heart,
And learn to embrace every fractured part,
For even in turmoil, there's beauty to find,
A testament to resilience, a spark of the mind.

In the depths of my struggle, I'll carve out my space,
A sanctuary built from the trials I face,
And though the demons may linger, I'll learn to be free,
For I am not my disorder; I am simply me.

Shadows of the Heart

In the theatre of my mind, the curtains draw tight,
A stage set for chaos, where day bleeds to night,
I stand in the spotlight, a marionette's dance,
Pulled by the strings of a heart's fragile chance.

In moments of comfort, the world feels so bright,
But shadows creep in, and they swallow the light,
With a flick of a thought, the colours all fade,
And I'm left in the silence, a masquerade.

It's all or it's nothing, a pendulum's swing,
Where love is a fortress, or a dagger's cruel sting,
I'm lost in the echoes of what could have been,
A prisoner of feelings, a battle within.

You were my sunrise, my laughter, my song,
But the moment you faltered, I felt it was wrong,
In the blink of an eye, you became the abyss,
A chasm of darkness where hope ceased to exist.

I split like the sky in a thunderous storm,
Where warmth turns to ice, and the heart feels so torn,
You're either my saviour or my greatest despair,
In this all-or-nothing, I'm gasping for air.

In quiet despair, the war rages on,
A tempest of thoughts, where the light has withdrawn,
I wear a brave mask, but inside I'm a child,
Lost in the shadows, both tender and wild.

I ache for connection, yet fear it will break,
A dance on the edge of a heart that won't wake,
For every sweet moment, a dagger will pierce,
And the love that I crave feels so distant, so fierce.

Oh, the weight of this splitting, it crushes my soul,
A cycle of longing that never feels whole,
I'm tethered to memories, both bitter and sweet,
In a world of extremes, I'm forever incomplete.

But in this abyss, I search for a thread,
A glimmer of hope in the words left unsaid,
For though I may falter, I yearn to believe,
That love can be gentle, that I can receive.

So I'll gather the pieces, the shards of my heart,
And learn to embrace every fractured part,
For in the depths of this struggle, I'll find my own way,
To bridge the divide, to live for today.

In the shadows of sorrow, I'll carve out my space,
A sanctuary built from the trials I face,
And though I may split, I'll learn to be whole,
For I am not just my pain; I am a beautiful soul.

The Mask I Wear

I stand before the world, a portrait of calm,
A serene façade, a soothing balm,
Yet beneath this stillness, a tempest does churn,
A fire of anguish, a lesson unlearned.

You see me smiling, a picture of grace,
But inside I'm a ghost in a desolate space,
With every heartbeat, a whisper of doubt,
A battle within that I cannot shout.

I crave for control, yet chaos is near,
The unknown looms large, and I tremble in fear,
I build up my walls, a fortress so high,
To shield from the storms that rage in the sky.

I withdraw from the light, retreat to the dark,
In silence I linger, a flickering spark,
Dissociation wraps me in its cold embrace,
A refuge from pain, a forgotten place.

Who am I, really? A question unasked,
A shadow of self, in a mask I am masked,
Low self-esteem whispers, "You're never enough,"
And I stumble through life, feeling broken and rough.

I carry the weight of a world on my back,
Blame myself for the cracks, for the love that I lack,
Self-sabotage dances, a cruel, twisted friend,
In the mirror, I see only a heart that won't mend.

I fear the conflict, the anger, the strife,
I tiptoe on eggshells, avoiding my life,
I check every word, every glance, every tone,
In the quest for connection, I feel so alone.

Abandonment looms like a shadowy ghost,
While intimacy feels like a perilous coast,
I long for the warmth of a hand in my own,
Yet I push you away, afraid of the known.

I look so perfect, a vision so bright,
But inside I'm crumbling, lost in the night,
Isolation wraps me in its suffocating shroud,
A silent scream trapped beneath a proud crowd.

Oh, the irony of this life that I lead,
A garden of thorns where I long for a seed,
To blossom, to flourish, to break through the pain,
To find in the chaos a reason to remain.

So here I stand, with my heart on my sleeve,
A tapestry woven with threads of believe,
For though I am fractured, I yearn to be whole,
To embrace every shadow, to nurture my soul.

In the depths of my struggle, I'll learn to be free,
To dance with my demons, to finally see,
That beneath all the layers, the hurt and the strife,
There's beauty in chaos, there's power in life.

The Depths of My Heart

In the shadows of my mind, a tempest brews,
A storm of emotions, a kaleidoscope of blues,
Borderline, they whisper, a label so stark,
Yet they cannot fathom the depths of this dark.

I wear my pain like a shroud, heavy and tight,
Each heartbeat a reminder of my endless fight,
For in this fragile vessel, emotions collide,
A symphony of anguish, where hope often hides.

Grief floods my soul, a river of despair,
Not just sadness, but a weight I can't bear,
It crashes like waves on a desolate shore,
A relentless reminder of what I abhor.

Shame wraps around me, a suffocating chain,
What once was a whisper now echoes as pain,
Humiliation dances, a cruel, mocking jest,
In a world that feels heavy, I long for some rest.

Rage ignites like wildfire, consuming my core,
What once was a flicker now rages for more,
Annoyance is a whisper, but fury's a scream,
In the chaos of feelings, I shatter the dream.

Panic grips me, a thief in the night,
Stealing my breath, extinguishing light,
Nervousness morphs into terror profound,
In the silence of solitude, I'm lost, never found.

Rejection's a dagger, it pierces so deep,
A wound that won't heal, a promise I keep,
Isolation's a prison, its bars made of fear,
In a crowd, I am lonely, in silence, I hear.

Perceived failure looms like a shadowy ghost,
A haunting reminder of what matters most,
I reach for connection, but it slips through my hands,
Like grains of fine sand, it escapes, it disbands.

Oh, the agony of feeling too much, too fast,
A heart that's a tempest, a die that's been cast,
In the depths of my sorrow, I search for a sign,
A glimmer of hope, a thread that's divine.

But here in this chaos, I find a strange grace,
A beauty in struggle, a light in the space,
For though I am fractured, I'm learning to see,
That the depths of my heart hold the key to be free.

So I'll rise from the ashes, though battered and torn,
With each tear that falls, a new strength is born,
For in this wild journey, I'll learn to embrace,
The tempest within me, the scars, and the grace.

The Weight of Being Real

In a world of shadows, where masks are worn,
I stand uncommonly real, where dreams are born.
Daringly genuine, I carve my own way,
With love like a wildfire, I seize every day.

I dive into moments, where the heartbeats collide,
In laughter and tears, I refuse to hide.
For this is my life, a canvas unframed,
Each stroke a reminder, I'm fiercely unchained.

No regrets in my pocket, no guilt on my sleeve,
I chase after purpose, in what I believe.
With every heartbeat, I dance with the light,
Embracing the darkness, I'm ready to fight.

But oh, how the world can be cruel and unkind,
When the heart that loves deeply is often maligned.
For in being so real, I've opened my chest,
To the weight of the world, and the pain of the rest.

I've loved with abandon, I've given my all,
Yet sometimes the echoes of silence can call.
In the depths of my soul, where the shadows creep in,
I wonder if being so real is a sin.

For the moments I cherish, the laughter, the grace,
Can vanish like whispers, leaving only a trace.
And the dreams that I chased, like fireflies in flight,
Can flicker and fade in the cold of the night.

So if you seek me, I'm out there, I swear,
Flying by the seat of my pants, unaware.
In a uniquely beautiful way, I'll remain,
But the weight of my truth can feel like a chain.

For every heart that I've touched, every soul that I've known,
Leaves a mark on my spirit, a seed that is sown.
And as I stand tall, with my heart on my sleeve,
I wonder if being so real is to grieve.

To love hard and deeply, to feel every ache,
To embrace every moment, for love's precious sake.
Yet in this vast journey, where the wild winds blow,
I'll carry my truth, though it cuts to the bone.

So here's to the dreamers, the lovers, the brave,
To the ones who are real, who refuse to be saved.
May we find in our hearts, a solace, a balm,
In the chaos of life, may we still find our calm.

For though it may crush us, this weight that we bear,
In the depths of our being, we're beautifully rare.
And if tears are the price for a life that is true,
Then let them fall freely, for I'll always choose you.

From Shadows to Strength: A Journey Reborn

I have been the stubborn bull,
Charging through life with a heart made of stone,
The ruthless snake, coiled tight in my skin,
A venomous whisper, a truth left alone.

I've been the dreaded disease,
A plague on my spirit, a burden of fate,
Each step a reminder of the misery I've walked,
Each breath a reminder of the weight I create.

In the depths where silence screams,
I wandered lost in shattered dreams,
A hollow shell, a fading light,
Each breath a battle, day and night.

I've depleted my soul in the depths of despair,
Butchered my body, a canvas of scars,
A testament to battles fought in the dark,
A map of my journey, a trail of my wars.

My body, a prison, heavy and cold,
Mirrors reflected a stranger's face,
Thoughts like daggers, sharp and cruel,
Whispered lies, I played the fool.

Struck with addiction, a thief in the night,
Littered with shame, I've hidden my face,
I've seen my share of trauma,
And danced with the demons that time can't erase.

"Give up," they taunted, "let darkness win,"
But deep inside, a flicker began to spin.
They called me insane, a label I wore,
A badge of my suffering, a crown of my pain.

Then came Jarrah Martin, a beacon bright,
With words that pierced the endless night,
"Your journey's not over, it's just begun,
Together we'll rise, we'll fight, we'll run."

In that first chat, a spark ignited,
A glimmer of hope, once so slighted,
He spoke of strength, of purpose, of grace,
A vision of life, a new embrace.

And then there was Rose Hamilton, my guiding star,
With plans and passion, she raised the bar,
Meal by meal, and step by step,
She held my hand, through every misstep.

At my lowest, when shadows loomed,
She stood beside me, my spirit resumed,
Celebrating victories, both big and small,
Her joy was a blanket, a comforting shawl.

(cont. next page)

But I will say this with passion,
I rise from the ashes, I break every chain,
I stitched my wounds with threads of my tears,
Each knot a reminder of the strength I've reclaimed.

With every workout, I shed the weight,
Not just of flesh, but of self-hate,
Each drop of sweat, a tear released,
In the forge of struggle, my soul found peace.

Now I stand, not just to survive,
But to thrive, to flourish, to truly arrive,
From rock bottom's grip, I've learned to ascend,
With Rose and Jarrah, my heart will mend.

So here I stand, a warrior of scars,
With a heart that beats fiercely, a soul that is free,
I've embraced my reflection, the good and the bad,
And in loving my truth, I've finally found me.

Let the world see my journey, let them witness my rise,
For the stubborn bull and the ruthless snake,
Are but fragments of me, a mosaic of life,
And in every piece shattered, a new path I make.

So if you feel broken, if you're lost in the night,
Know that the shadows can lead you to light,
For we are all warriors, with stories to tell,
And in the depths of our struggles, we learn how to dwell.

Let the tears fall like rain, let them wash us anew,
For in the heart of our battles, we find what is true.
And though I've been burdened, I rise from the pain,
With love as my armour, I'll dance in the rain.

So here's to the journey, the battles we face,
To the strength found in love, in kindness, in grace,
From shadows to strength, I rise and I soar,
With every heartbeat, I'm ready for more.

Ink and Ashes

In the dawn's grey light, I rise,
A weary soul with heavy sighs,
The world outside, a distant dream,
While I am caught in a silent scream.

Seven years lost in a haze of despair,
Chasing shadows, gasping for air,
Addiction's grip, a relentless thief,
Stealing my joy, my hope, my belief.

But now, I stand, 512 days free,
A fragile victory, a new part of me,
The chains that once bound me, now lie in the past,
In the ashes of struggle, I've found strength at last.

The walls around me, peeling paint,
Echo whispers of hope, now faint,
Each day a battle, each breath a fight,
In the grip of darkness, I search for light.

With pen in hand, I pour out my soul,
Each word a step toward a distant goal,
I scribble my pain on the pages of night,
Transforming my anguish into something bright.

I write of the battles, the demons I face,
Of nights spent in silence, in a desolate place,
Of cravings that claw at the edges of mind,
In the rhythm of verses, my solace I find.

I pen down my fears, my hopes, my despair,
In the ink of my struggles, I lay my soul bare,
For if I can share this, if someone can see,
Then perhaps in my words, they'll find a key.

A key to unlock the chains of their mind,
To know they're not alone, that they too can find,
A path through the darkness, a way to be free,
In the stories of others, we find unity.

I dream of a book, of pages that turn,
Of hearts that will open, of souls that will yearn,
To feel the connection, to know they are seen,
In the tapestry woven from all that has been.

So here I stand, with my ink and my pain,
A man forged in struggle, yet willing to gain,
For every small victory, I'll cherish and hold,
A testament written in stories untold.

And one day, I'll rise, from this pit of despair,
With the strength of a thousand, I'll breathe in the air,
No longer a prisoner, no longer confined,
A poet, a warrior, with a spirit aligned.

So let the world see, let the world know,
That even in darkness, a seed can still grow,
For I am a writer, though weary and worn,
In the depths of my sorrow, a new life is born.

With every word written, I reach for the light,
In the ink of my ashes, I find my own fight,
And if my book touches just one lonely heart,
Then I'll know my struggle was a beautiful start.

Kill Them with Success

In the quiet shadows where dreams lay to rest,
I've walked through the valleys, I've faced every test,
With scars on my heart and ashes in hand,
I rise from the ruins, I take my stand.

Kill them with success, they said with a sneer,
As if triumph could silence the echoes of fear,
But success is a mountain, steep and unkind,
A summit of sorrow, where hope's hard to find.

I've tasted the bitterness, the salt of my tears,
Each drop a reminder of all of my years,
Of battles fought fiercely, of nights spent alone,
Of whispers that haunted, of seeds that were sown.

Bury them with a smile, they said with disdain,
As if joy could erase all the heartache and pain,
But smiles can be masks, worn thin and frayed,
Hiding the tempest, the price that I've paid.

For every triumph, a shadow looms near,
A ghost of the past, a whisper of fear,
And in the stillness, when the world turns away,
I grapple with demons that refuse to stay.

I've climbed every mountain, I've conquered each foe,
Yet the weight of my journey is heavy to tow,
For success is a burden, a crown made of thorns,
A testament forged in the fires of scorn.

So I stand here, trembling, with tears in my eyes,
A warrior of heart, beneath unforgiving skies,
And I'll kill them with success, but not with a grin,
For the battle is fierce, and the war rages within.

I'll bury them with a smile, but it won't be bright,
It'll be the kind born from the depths of the night,
A smile that knows sorrow, that carries the weight,
Of dreams that were shattered, of love turned to hate.

And as I rise, I'll remember the cost,
The pieces of me that I thought I had lost,
For in every victory, there's a price to be paid,
A heart that is heavy, a spirit that's frayed.

So let them all watch as I claim what is mine,
With a heart full of courage, and a soul that will shine,
But know that behind every triumph I wear,
Is a story of struggle, a burden to bear.

In the end, it's not just the success that I seek,
But the strength to be human, to rise when I'm weak,
To embrace all the shadows, to dance in the rain,
To find beauty in heartache, to grow from the pain.

So I'll kill them with success, and bury them deep,
With a smile that carries the secrets I keep,
For in every tear shed, in every wound healed,
Lies the power of truth, the strength of the real.

And if my heart breaks, let it break wide open,
For in the fragments, my spirit is woven,
A tapestry rich with the colours of strife,
A testament written to the beauty of life.

Echoes of the Soul

In the stillness of a fading day,
Where shadows stretch and whispers play,
I stand alone, a heart laid bare,
With echoes of love that linger in the air.

Once, your laughter danced like light,
A melody that chased away the night,
But now, the silence wraps me tight,
A shroud of memories, lost from sight.

I reach for you in dreams that fade,
In every corner where our laughter played,
Yet all I grasp is empty space,
A haunting void, a ghostly trace.

The warmth of your hand, the spark in your eyes,
Now just a flicker, a distant sigh,
I wander through the halls of our past,
Each echo a reminder, a shadow cast.

Time, the thief, with its cruel embrace,
Stole the moments, erased your face,
Yet in the depths of my aching soul,
Your essence lingers, a bittersweet whole.

I wear my grief like a tattered cloak,
Each thread a word, each stitch a choke,
For love, once vibrant, now draped in grey,
Is a song unsung, a price to pay.

But in this sorrow, a flicker remains,
A testament to joy, a dance through the pain,
For every tear that falls like rain,
Is an echo of love, a whisper of gain.

So I gather the fragments, the shards of our song,
And weave them together, where they belong,
In the tapestry of my heart, you'll forever reside,
An echo of the soul, my eternal guide.

Though the world may crumble, and shadows may fall,
Your spirit will rise, through it all,
For love is a journey, a winding road,
And in every echo, your memory glowed.

So I'll listen closely, in the quiet of night,
To the echoes of you, my heart's guiding light,
For though you are gone, you're never far,
In the depths of my soul, you're my brightest star.

Whispers of the Forgotten

In the quiet corners of a fading room,
Where shadows linger, and memories loom,
A child once laughed, with dreams in her eyes,
Now echoes of silence, where hope slowly dies.

Her teddy bear worn, with stitches undone,
Holds secrets of laughter, of battles once won,
But time is a thief, with a heart made of stone,
It steals all the moments, leaves us alone.

A mother's soft lullaby, now a ghost in the air,
Each note a reminder of love's cruel despair,
She cradled her baby, with warmth in her heart,
Now the cradle is empty, torn worlds fall apart.

The father, once strong, with hands built of steel,
Now trembles in shadows, his wounds never heal,
He whispers her name to the stars up above,
But the night swallows echoes of unending love.

In the garden they planted, where flowers once bloomed,
Now weeds choke the laughter, and silence consumes,
Each petal that falls is a tear from the sky,
A reminder of moments that withered and died.

And the world keeps on turning, indifferent and cold,
While hearts break in silence, their stories untold,
For every lost dream, for each shattered sigh,
There's a universe weeping, a million goodbyes.

So hold close the fleeting, the fragile, the dear,
For time is a thief, and it steals what we fear,
In the tapestry woven with threads of our pain,
We find strength in the sorrow, and beauty in rain.

Let the tears flow like rivers, let the heartache be known,
For in every lost moment, we're never alone,
In the whispers of the forgotten, in the shadows of night,
We find love in the darkness, and hope in the light.

In the Shadow of Awakening

In the cradle of night, where silence weeps,
A soul is forged in the furnace of grief,
Each tear a testament, each scar a story,
In the depths of despair, we seek our glory.

The weight of the world, a shroud on the heart,
Each heartbeat a whisper, a world torn apart,
In the echo of anguish, the spirit takes flight,
For only through darkness can we find the light.

Oh, the burden of sorrow, the ache of the past,
A tapestry woven with shadows so vast,
The laughter of children, now ghosts in the air,
Their smiles like sunbeams, now lost in despair.

We wander through valleys where hope seems to die,
With dreams like fragile glass, shattered in the sky,
Yet in every fracture, a glimmer remains,
A flicker of courage that dances through pain.

For the evolved souls, the bearers of scars,
They cradle the darkness, they reach for the stars,
They study the shadows, the depths of the night,
To become the soft lanterns that guide us to light.

But oh, the cost of this luminous grace,
Is a heart that has bled in the cruelest of places,
A spirit that's weathered the storms of despair,
With love that is heavy, yet tender and rare.

So when you see light in a stranger's kind eyes,
Know it's born from the ashes of countless goodbyes,
From the depths of their suffering, they rise to ignite,
A beacon of hope in the long, endless night.

And as we gather, our stories entwined,
In the tapestry woven of hearts that have pined,
Let us honour the darkness, the pain that we share,
For in every soul's journey, there's beauty laid bare.

So we weep for the lost, for the dreams that have flown,
For the love that was shattered, for the seeds that were sown,
In the garden of sorrow, where shadows take root,
We find the resilience, the strength to bear fruit.

In the depth of our trials, we learn to embrace,
The light that emerges from suffering's face,
For the depth of our awakening, the truth we must see,
Is that through our own darkness, we set others free.

The Weight of Unseen Waters

I've spoiled too many, like flowers in frost,
Gave my heart to the hollow, my warmth to the lost,
I carved out my essence, a map of my soul,
For those who would never, not once, make me whole.

I crossed oceans for shadows, for whispers of dreams,
While they danced in the daylight, I drowned in their schemes,
I poured out my spirit, like wine on the ground,
For the unworthy to sip, while my own heart was bound.

Oh, the weight of the choices, the burdens I bore,
The echoes of laughter that turned into war,
I stood in the rain, with my heart on my sleeve,
While they turned their backs, I learned how to grieve.

I no longer chase phantoms, nor run after ghosts,
For the love that I offered was met with mere boasts,
I've learned that my worth is not measured in pain,
That the oceans I crossed were in vain, all in vain.

Yet in the stillness, a whisper breaks through,
A promise of solace, a love that is true,
For there are hands waiting, with warmth and with grace,
Who would leap through the storms, who would cherish my place.

I see them now, glimmers in the dark,
Those souls who would journey, who'd light up the spark,
They'd hold me through tempests, through trials and fears,
And together we'd dance, through the laughter and tears.

So I gather my pieces, reclaim what is mine,
No more will I settle for love that's unkind,
I'll build my own bridges, I'll chart my own seas,
With those who would jump over puddles with ease.

For the heart that is tender, the spirit that's bright,
Deserves not the shadows, but the warmth of the light,
And though I've been broken, I rise from the fall,
With the strength of the ocean, I'll answer the call.

So here's to the journey, to the love that is real,
To the hands that will hold me, to the hearts that will heal,
I'll no longer be anchored by those who won't see,
For I'm crossing my oceans, and I'm finally free.

The Mirror of Despair

No, don't tell me, "You attract what you are,"
As if kindness alone could mend every scar.
What if I'm gentle, yet shadows draw near,
What if my light only deepens their fear?

What if I'm honest, with truth in my veins,
Yet I'm met with the liars, the masters of games?
What if my loyalty, a beacon so bright,
Is met with betrayal, in the dead of the night?

No, it's not always the mirror that shows,
The reflection of goodness, the beauty that grows.
Sometimes it's chaos, it's heartache and pain,
That finds its way home, like a moth to the flame.

I've given my heart to the broken and bruised,
To those who would take, leaving me feeling used.
I've wrapped my compassion around their despair,
While they danced in my kindness, unaware, unaware.

What if I'm a garden, with blossoms in bloom,
Yet I'm trampled by footsteps that darken the room?
What if my laughter, a song in the air,
Is drowned by the silence of those who don't care?

I've stood in the fire, my spirit ablaze,
While they fed on my warmth, lost in their haze.
I've opened my arms to the lost and the torn,
Only to find that my heart was worn.

What if I'm a lighthouse, guiding the lost,
Yet they crash on the rocks, never counting the cost?
What if my kindness is a beacon of hope,
Yet they tether my heart with their fragile rope?

No, you don't always attract what you are,
Sometimes you're a saviour, yet they leave you ajar.
You draw in the desperate, the broken, the weak,
And they feast on your spirit, while you're left to seek.

But in the depths of this sorrow, a truth starts to rise,
That even in darkness, there's light in the skies.
For every heart shattered, there's one that will mend,
And the love that you give will return in the end.

So I'll gather my pieces, I'll stand tall and proud,
I'll embrace all the kindness, I'll shout it out loud.
For though I attract those who need what I give,
I'll find my own tribe, and together we'll live.

No, don't tell me "You attract what you are,"
For I'll shine through the pain, I'll reach for the stars.
And in the tapestry woven from heartache and grace,
I'll find those who cherish the light in my face.

Echoes of Resilience

In the shadows where the lost souls dwell,
He wandered through the echoes of his hell,
A heart once vibrant, now a hollow shell,
Riddled with scars, a story hard to tell.

Each night a battle, each dawn a retreat,
With demons that danced on his weary feet,
Addiction's embrace, a cold, cruel deceit,
In the alleys of anguish, he faced his defeat.

He wore his past like a tattered shroud,
A canvas of violence, a life unbowed,
Shot and stabbed, robbed of hope, lost in the crowd,
Homeless more times than he dared to say aloud.

The whispers of darkness, they beckoned him near,
A symphony of sorrow, a chorus of fear,
Yet deep in his heart, a flicker appeared,
A longing for solace, a voice that was clear.

"Help me," he whispered, through tears and despair,
To Inspire Mindful Psychology, he laid himself bare,
Dr Merima Isakovic, with compassion to share,
Took his shattered pieces, crafted them with care.

With patience like rivers, she guided his way,
Through valleys of shadows, to the light of the day,
At his own pace, she helped him to stay,
To rise from the ashes, to find words to say.

Days turned to months, and the chains fell away,
512 days clean, he learned how to play,
With ink in his veins, he found strength in the fray,
A phoenix reborn, in the dawn's gentle ray.

Now he pens his truth, with a heart open wide,
In "Ink and Ashes," he no longer hides,
Each poem a testament, where hope abides,
A journey from darkness, where love now resides.

So let the world weep for the battles he fought,
For the moments of silence, the lessons he taught,
In the tapestry woven from pain that he sought,
He found his redemption, in the love that he caught.

For every soul wandering, lost in the night,
There's a path to the dawn, a flicker of light,
With courage to reach out, to stand up and fight,
Inspire Mindful Psychology, a beacon so bright.

So read his words softly, let the tears flow,
For in every line, there's a story to know,
Of a man who emerged from the depths of his woe,
With ink and with ashes, he learned how to grow.

Whispers of Strength

In the depths of despair, where shadows conspire,
He wandered through hell, consumed by the fire,
A heart once alive, now a ghost in the mire,
Riddled with addiction, a soul lost to the choir.

Each night was a battle, each dawn a cruel jest,
With demons that whispered, "You'll never find rest,"
Shot and stabbed, robbed of hope, feeling less,
Homeless more times than he dared to confess.

But the darkest of nights brought a shattering call,
A voice from the void, a friend's final fall,
Jack Aaron Neal, his soulmate, his all,
Brutally taken, leaving echoes that crawl.

His world fell apart, like glass on the floor,
Each shard a reminder of what was before,
Grief wrapped around him, a suffocating score,
In the silence of sorrow, he couldn't take more.

Yet in the abyss, a flicker of light,
A name whispered softly, breaking the night,
Linda Usope, a medium, a guide in his plight,
With wisdom and kindness, she brought forth the sight.

Through tears and through tremors, she helped him to see,
That love never dies, it's a bond, wild and free,
She reached through the darkness, showed him how to be,
A vessel of hope, where despair used to be.

With each gentle session, she pieced him anew,
Helped him face grief, let the memories through,
Saw the good in his heart when the world only blew,
In the depths of his sorrow, she painted a view.

"Your future is waiting," she whispered with grace,
"Beyond all the shadows, there's a light you can chase,
Though the pain feels eternal, it's not your only place,
You're worthy of love, of joy, and embrace."

So he gathered the fragments, the ashes of pain,
With Linda beside him, he learned to sustain,
The love of his soulmate, a bond that won't wane,
In the tapestry woven, he found strength in the rain.

Now he walks with a purpose, a heart open wide,
With Jack in his spirit, he carries the pride,
From the depths of his sorrow, he's learned to abide,
In the echoes of love, where hope will reside.

So let the world witness this journey of grace,
From the pits of despair to a brighter embrace,
For in every heartbeat, in every soft trace,
There's a story of healing, a life to embrace.

In the ashes of loss, he found a new song,
With Linda's compassion, he learned to be strong,
For every soul shattered, for every heart wronged,
There's a path to the light, where the lost can belong.

Threads of Endurance

In the quiet corners of a restless mind,
Where shadows dance and hope is blind,
A tempest brews, a silent scream,
A fragile heart, unravelling seam by seam.

Each dawn arrives with a heavy shroud,
A sun that rises, yet feels so loud,
The weight of existence, a leaden chain,
In a world of colour, I see only pain.

I wear a mask, a painted smile,
But beneath the surface, I've walked a mile,
Through valleys of doubt, through forests of fear,
Where demons whisper, "No one is near."

They claw at my spirit, they gnaw at my soul,
In the depths of despair, I've lost all control,
"Just let go," they murmur, "find peace in the night,
In the stillness of darkness, you'll find your light."

But what of the love that I leave in the wake?
The laughter of children, the bonds that won't break?
The echoes of voices that once filled my heart,
Now fade into silence, as I drift apart.

I think of the moments, the joy and the pain,
The warmth of a hug, the soft summer rain,
Yet here in this battle, I'm weary and worn,
A soldier of sorrow, forever forlorn.

I reach for the stars, but they slip through my hands,
A universe vast, with uncharted lands,
And I'm just a whisper, a flicker, a sigh,
A ghost in the shadows, too tired to fly.

But in the abyss, a flicker remains,
A glimmer of hope, through the shackles and chains,
A voice that calls softly, "You're not alone,
In the depths of your struggle, you're still being known."

So I'll fight through the darkness, I'll claw through the night,
For the love that surrounds me, for the flickering light,
For the laughter of children, the warmth of a friend,
In the tapestry woven, I'll find my own thread.

And though the demons may whisper, may howl and may scream,
I'll hold onto the fragments, the remnants of dreams,
For life is a journey, a winding, rough road,
And in every heartbeat, I'll carry my load.

So here's to the fighters, the weary, the brave,
To the souls who are drowning, yet still try to save,
In the depths of despair, let us rise and reclaim,
For the beauty of living is worth all the pain.

Echoes of the Forgotten

In the stillness of twilight, a whisper calls my name,
A scent drifts through the shadows, igniting an old flame.
The air, thick with sorrow, a bittersweet embrace,
I'm pulled into the tempest of a long-lost, haunted place.

The musk of dampened earth, where blood once stained the ground,
A symphony of silence, where the echoes still resound.
I close my eyes, and suddenly, the past comes rushing back,
A kaleidoscope of memories, a heart under attack.

I see the faces, weary, etched with lines of pain,
Brothers turned to strangers, in a world of loss and gain.
Their laughter now a ghost, their dreams a distant star,
Each heartbeat like a cannon, each breath a battle scar.

The thunder of the cannons, the cries that pierced the night,
The weight of heavy burdens, the struggle for the right.
I smell the smoke of anguish, the fear that filled the air,
A tapestry of heartache, woven with despair.

Oh, how the memories flood, like rivers in the rain,
Each flashback a reminder of the love entwined with pain.
I see the fields of sorrow, where hope was laid to rest,
And feel the heartache rising, a relentless, aching chest.

My heart races like a soldier, caught in a fray of time,
Each pulse a drum of anguish, each beat a mournful rhyme.
I'm lost within the echoes, where shadows dance and play,
In the theatre of the broken, where the light has turned to grey.

The scent of war still lingers, a ghost that will not fade,
A reminder of the battles, the choices that we made.
And in this haunting moment, I'm tethered to the past,
A soul crushed by the memories, a love that couldn't last.

So here I stand, a witness, to the stories left untold,
To the hearts that beat in silence, to the dreams that turned to gold.
In the depths of my remembrance, I find both peace and strife,
For in the scent of war, I breathe the essence of life.

And though the tears may fall, like rain upon the ground,
I carry forth their whispers, in the silence, they resound.
For every soul that suffered, for every heart that bled,
In the echoes of the forgotten, their legacy is spread.

To My Little Girl

How do I tell the woman who stands before me now,
The depths of my heart, the weight of my vow?
You are my daughter, my pride, my delight,
My best friend, my compass, my guiding light.

In the tapestry of time, woven with care,
You are the thread that sparkles, the breath of fresh air.
You are my life, my laughter, my song,
Yet above all these things, you are where I belong.

Oh, my little girl, with dreams in your eyes,
In your laughter, I hear the soft echoes of skies.
Though the years have flown by, like whispers in flight,
When I look at you now, I still see my light.

I could say that I love you, but words fall so short,
For love is a river, and you are its port.
You are everything to me, my heart's gentle plea,
The first thing I thank God for, each morning I see.

And as twilight descends, with shadows that creep,
You are the last thought that lingers, the promise I keep.
In the silence of night, when the world fades away,
It's your smile that guides me, come what may.

But time, oh cruel time, with its relentless embrace,
Steals moments like treasures, leaves only a trace.
I watch as you blossom, as you spread your wings wide,
Yet a part of me trembles, a part of me hides.

For the little girl's laughter, the soft, tender sighs,
Are now echoes of memories, like stars in the skies.
And though I am proud, my heart aches with the cost,
For each step that you take, I feel a piece lost.

So how do I tell you, as you stand here today,
That you are my everything, in every way?
That the love that I carry, so deep and so true,
Is a river of sorrow, a joy born of you.

In the dance of our lives, as the seasons unfold,
Know that you are my treasure, more precious than gold.
And though the years may take you, and the world may demand,
You'll always be my little girl, forever my hand.

So here's to the moments, both bitter and sweet,
To the laughter, the tears, to the love that we meet.
For in every heartbeat, in every soft sigh,
You are my forever, my reason to fly.

And when the day comes, when I must let you go,
Remember, my darling, you're the love that I know.
You are my daughter, my best friend, my life,
And in the depths of my soul, you'll always be my light.

Whispers of Jack

I know Jack is with me, each dawn's gentle light,
In the rustle of leaves, in the hush of the night,
He makes sure to linger, a ghost in my day,
A whisper of love that won't fade away.

Yet it's not the same, this tether we share,
For the warmth of his presence is a weight I must bear,
I love having him close, in the shadows he glows,
But the ache in my heart is a wound that still grows.

I miss his hugs, those embraces so tight,
The way he would hold me, make everything right,
In the depths of my sorrow, when the world felt so cold,
His smile was a beacon, a story retold.

Oh, how I miss him, that light in his eyes,
The laughter that danced like the stars in the skies,
His smile, a sunrise that banished my night,
A balm for my spirit, a spark of pure light.

Now I wander through memories, a ghost of the past,
In the echoes of laughter, in shadows that cast,
I reach for his presence, but find only air,
A longing that grips me, a love laid so bare.

Each moment I cherish, each memory I hold,
Is a thread in the tapestry, a story retold,
Yet the fabric is fraying, the colours now dim,
For the heart that once thrived now beats on a whim.

I miss him, I whisper, to the stars up above,
To the winds that still carry the scent of his love,
In the silence that follows, in the tears that I cry,
I search for his spirit, I reach for the sky.

But in every soft breeze, in the rustle of trees,
I feel him beside me, in the sigh of the leaves,
He's the warmth in my heart, the strength in my soul,
Yet the void that he left is a chasm, a hole.

So I carry his memory, a treasure so dear,
In the laughter of children, in the songs that I hear,
For though he is gone, he's forever my guide,
In the love that we shared, in the tears that I've cried.

I know Jack is with me, in the light and the dark,
In the moments of silence, in the flicker of sparks,
Yet I ache for his presence, for the warmth of his smile,
For the hugs that would carry me over each mile.

So I'll hold onto love, though the pain cuts so deep,
In the whispers of Jack, in the dreams that I keep,
For though he is distant, he's never truly gone,
In the heart of my sorrow, his spirit lives on.

In the Shadows of Ink

In a world where nothing was as it seems,
Where laughter echoed like distant dreams,
I wandered through halls of whispered disdain,
An outsider, a ghost, lost in the rain.

Weird, they called me, a freak in their eyes,
Stupid, they said, as I wore my disguise.
Each word a dagger, each glance a stone,
In the silence of crowds, I felt so alone.

But in the stillness, when night draped its veil,
I found a refuge where my heart could exhale.
With ink as my lifeline, I bared my soul,
In verses and stanzas, I began to feel whole.

Poetry, my saviour, my solace, my song,
In the rhythm of heartbeats, I finally belonged.
Each line a confession, each rhyme a release,
In the chaos of life, I discovered my peace.

I painted my pain with the colours of truth,
Unravelled my fears, reclaimed my lost youth.
With every word woven, I stitched up my heart,
In the tapestry of language, I found my own art.

But the world outside, it still turned its back,
And shadows of doubt would creep in, attack.
For every bright stanza, a chorus of jeers,
For every sweet triumph, a flood of my tears.

Yet still, I wrote on, through the darkness and light,
For in every struggle, I found my own fight.
With ink-stained fingers, I carved out my name,
In the book of existence, I'd never be the same.

So here I stand, with my heart on my sleeve,
A testament to all who dare to believe.
That in the depths of despair, where hope seems to fade,
There's power in words, in the love that we've made.

And if you feel lost, like a ship in the storm,
Know that in your own verses, you too can transform.
For poetry breathes where silence once lay,
It's the light in the shadows, the dawn of the day.

So let the tears flow, let them wash you anew,
For in every heartache, there's beauty in you.
In a world where nothing is ever as it seems,
You are the poet, the dreamer of dreams.

Three Years Without You

In the quiet of the morning, where shadows softly creep,
I trace the lines of memories, where laughter used to leap.
Three years have slipped like whispers, through fingers cold and bare,
Yet every breath I take is laced with the weight of despair.

You were the sun in my sky, the anchor in my storm,
A heartbeat in the silence, a shelter safe and warm.
But fate, with cruel intentions, tore you from my embrace,
Left me to wander aimlessly, in this desolate space.

I never got to say goodbye, to hold you one last time,
To tell you how you changed me, how you made my spirit climb.
Now I'm haunted by the echoes of words I never spoke,
Each syllable a dagger, each silence like a choke.

The demons come at twilight, they whisper in my ear,
They tell me I'm forgotten, that you're no longer near.
But in the depths of sorrow, I feel your presence still,
A flicker in the darkness, a testament of will.

I see you in the raindrops, in the stars that light the night,
In every fleeting moment, in every fragile fight.
Yet the ache of your absence is a wound that never heals,
A chasm deep and endless, where love and longing kneels.

Three years of hollow laughter, three years of silent screams,
Three years of chasing shadows, of shattering my dreams.
I wear your memory like armour, though it cuts into my skin,
A bittersweet reminder of the love that lies within.

So here I stand, a soldier, in this battle with my heart,
Fighting through the memories, though they tear my soul apart.
I'll carry you forever, in the depths of who I am,
A love that knows no boundaries, a bond that time can't dam.

And though the world keeps turning, and life moves on its way,
I'll hold you in my heart, where you'll forever stay.
For every tear I shed, for every whispered prayer,
Is a testament to love, a promise to be there.

So on this day of sorrow, I'll light a candle bright,
To honour all the moments, to cherish all the light.
For you are not forgotten, you live within my soul,
And though the pain is heavy, it's your love that makes me whole.

In the Weight of Absence

In the echo of the gym, where our laughter used to soar,
I find the ghosts of memories, haunting every door.
Jack, you were my brother, in sweat and in the grind,
A bond forged in the iron, a love that intertwined.

March ninth, twenty twenty-two, the day the world stood still,
The weight of loss is heavy, a void I cannot fill.
You were the spark beside me, the fire in my soul,
Now every rep is a reminder of the part that's lost control.

The clang of metal echoes, a symphony of pain,
Each lift a bitter struggle, each breath a silent strain.
I see your face in shadows, in the mirrors of my mind,
A smile that lit the darkness, a spirit unconfined.

But now the gym is heaven, where our dreams once took flight,
And hell, where every heartbeat feels like a desperate fight.
I push against the demons, the grief that pulls me down,
In every drop of sweat, I wear your memory like a crown.

You taught me strength was more than just the weight we bore,
It was the heart behind the muscle, the love that we explore.
Yet here I stand, a warrior, with armour cracked and worn,
Fighting through the echoes of a bond forever torn.

The laughter we shared lingers, like a ghost in every space,
And every time I lift, I feel the absence of your grace.
I search for you in every corner, in the rhythm of the fight,
But all I find is silence, in the shadows of the night.

Jack, you were my anchor, my compass in the storm,
Now I'm lost in this vast ocean, where the waves of sorrow swarm.
I lift the weight of memories, each one a heavy stone,
And in this sacred temple, I feel so all alone.

But I will carry on, my brother, I will honour what we shared,
In every drop of effort, in every moment bared.
For you are in the heartbeat of the iron that I lift,
In the strength of every struggle, in the love that is our gift.

So here's to you, dear Jack, in every tear I cry,
In the gym where we once thrived, I'll keep your spirit high.
For though the pain is crushing, and the demons often call,
I'll rise, I'll fight, I'll remember, and I'll carry you through it all.

Echoes of Absence

In the quiet dawn, where shadows creep,
I wake to a world that feels too deep.
The sun rises slow, but it brings no light,
For the heart that once danced is now lost in night.

Mum, it's starting to hit me, the weight of your flight,
A silence so heavy, it swallows the light.
I thought I could handle this grief, this despair,
But the truth is a monster, too heavy to bear.

Each morning I wake, with hope in my chest,
Expecting your message, your love, your best.
But the phone lies still, no whispers, no calls,
Just echoes of laughter that bounce off the walls.

How do I go on, when the world feels so wrong?
When the heart that once sang, now just hums a sad song?
I reach for the memories, but they slip through my hands,
Like grains of soft sand, like forgotten plans.

You were my anchor, my compass, my guide,
Now I'm lost in the tempest, with nowhere to hide.
The warmth of your smile, the comfort of your touch,
Now haunt me like shadows, I miss you so much.

I see you in dreams, where the laughter is bright,
But I wake to the silence, to the cold, empty night.
The world keeps on turning, but I'm stuck in this place,
Where the love that we shared has left an empty space.

Oh, how do I breathe when the air feels so thick?
When the heartache is sharp, and the clock ticks so quick?
I'm scared of the future, of days without you,
Of moments unshared, of a life that feels blue.

But I'll carry your spirit, I'll hold it so tight,
In the depths of my sorrow, you'll be my light.
Though the pain is a river that flows through my soul,
I'll learn to keep living, to find a new whole.

So here's to the mornings, where I'll whisper your name,
To the love that won't fade, to the heart that still flames.
Though you're gone from my sight, you're forever my song,
In the echoes of absence, I'll learn to be strong.

Whispers of Absence

Today the sun rises, but shadows fall deep,
For today is your birthday, and I'm left here to weep.
The world spins around me, but I stand still in time,
Each tick of the clock is a chime of your rhyme.

I remember the laughter, the warmth of your smile,
The way you held my hand, made every moment worthwhile.
You were my compass, my anchor, my light,
Now I wander in darkness, lost in the night.

The cake sits untouched, the candles unlit,
Each flicker of flame is a memory I can't quit.
I whisper your name to the stars up above,
Hoping they carry my message, my love.

Oh, how I long for your voice, soft and clear,
To tell me I'm cherished, to wipe away fear.
But silence surrounds me, a blanket of pain,
As I count all the moments that will never remain.

I see you in flowers, in the breeze that I feel,
In the songs of the birds, in the love that is real.
Yet, it's not quite enough, this bittersweet grace,
For nothing can fill the void of your embrace.

I search for your laughter in the echoes of time,
In the corners of memories, in the rhythm of rhyme.
But today, dear mother, the world feels so cold,
As I carry your spirit, a treasure untold.

So I'll light a candle, let it flicker and sway,
A beacon of love on this heart-wrenching day.
And though you are gone, you're forever my guide,
In the depths of my sorrow, your love will abide.

Happy birthday, dear mother, in heaven so bright,
I'll hold you in my heart, through the long, lonely night.
For you were my world, my joy, and my song,
And in every tear shed, I know you belong.

So I'll celebrate you, though the ache never fades,
In the tapestry of life, your love never frays.
With each passing year, I'll remember and cry,
For today is your birthday, and I'm missing you, why?

"Whispers of a Grandmother's Heart"

In the quiet of a fading day,
A message sent, a heart laid bare,
Words wrapped in love, in hope, in prayer,
From a grandmother's soul, in a world of grey.

"Dear sweet child, I think of you,
In every breath, in every sigh,
I long to hear your laughter, too,
To see the sparkle in your eye."

But silence fell like a heavy shroud,
A ghost of words, a whisper lost,
The distance grew, the heartache loud,
A bridge unbuilt, a love embossed.

She watched the screen, her heart a drum,
Each tick of time, a cruel refrain,
The longing deep, the silence numb,
A love unspoken, a world of pain.

Days turned to nights, and nights to years,
Her heart, a vessel of uncried tears,
Each moment passed, a wish ungranted,
A bond unformed, a love supplanted.

And when the shadows claimed her light,
She held her dreams, her hopes, her fears,
In the stillness of that endless night,
She whispered softly, "My dear, my dear."

But the echoes faded, the stars grew dim,
A final breath, a gentle sigh,
A love that lingered, a love that brimmed,
Yet never found the chance to fly.

Now in the silence, a heart still aches,
For words unsaid, for paths untrod,
A legacy of love that time forsakes,
A bond unbroken, though she's gone to God.

So hold her close, in memory's embrace,
Let her spirit dance in your laughter's glow,
For in your heart, she finds her place,
In every tear, in every woe.

And though the message may never be sent,
Know that love transcends the silent space,
In every heartbeat, her soul is lent,
A grandmother's love, a timeless grace.

In the Echo
of Your Heart

In the quiet of the night, where shadows softly creep,
I find the echoes of your love, in memories I keep.
A tender thread of sorrow, woven deep in time,
For Zoran, your sweet boy, lost before his prime.

Two years, a fleeting moment, yet a lifetime in your soul,
A fragile heart now shattered, a wound that won't be whole.
You held him close, your sunshine, your laughter in the air,
But fate, with cruel hands, took him, leaving only despair.

And now, dear Mum, I see the truth, a mirror to your pain,
In the absence of your Zoran, your heart was left in rain.
When Michelle came into being, a flicker of that light,
You saw in her the echoes of your boy, lost to the night.

Each message that you sent her, a whisper from your heart,
A bridge across the silence, a longing to restart.
But silence met your yearning, and the distance grew so wide,
As she read your words of love, and turned away inside.

Oh, how it must have shattered, to feel that empty space,
To see your hopes reflected, yet never find her face.
For every word unspoken, for every tear you cried,
Was a testament to love, and the grief you could not hide.

Now I stand here, in the shadows, with the weight of what I know,
The love you poured for Zoran, the seeds of pain you sowed.
And in the distance from Michelle, I feel your heart's refrain,
A symphony of sorrow, a melody of pain.

So here's to you, my mother, with your heart so vast and wide,
For every child you cherished, for every tear you cried.
In the tapestry of loss, we find the threads of love,
And though the world may shatter, we'll rise with wings above.

Though Zoran has departed, Michelle stands apart,
We carry her in our hearts, though we're now estranged.
In the garden of our memories, their echoes still impart.

So let the tears fall freely, let the heartache find its way,
For in the depths of sorrow, we find the light of day.
In every whispered memory, in every silent prayer,
We hold you close, dear mother, in the love we all still share.

Six Months Without You

Six months today, the clock ticks slow,
Each second a reminder of the love I know,
A world once vibrant, now draped in grey,
Since you left, dear Mum, I've lost my way.

Your laughter, a melody, now echoes in dreams,
A haunting refrain, unravelling at the seams,
I reach for the moments, the warmth of your hand,
But grasp only shadows, like grains of sand.

I've climbed every mountain, I've chased every star,
Yet every triumph feels hollow, for you're not where you are,
I've painted my victories in colours so bright,
But the canvas is empty without your guiding light.

I miss you more than words can ever convey,
In the silence of night, I long for your sway,
The stories you told, the wisdom you shared,
Now linger like whispers, in a heart that's ensnared.

I've achieved so much, yet it's bittersweet,
For every success feels like a retreat,
I wish you could see me, I wish you could know,
That your love was the seed from which I did grow.

Six months today, and the ache never fades,
In the garden of grief, where memory cascades,
I gather the petals of moments we had,
And weave them together, both joyful and sad.

Oh, Mum, if you're watching, if you're somehow near,
Know that your spirit is forever held dear,
In the depths of my heart, you'll always reside,
A love everlasting, my eternal guide.

So I'll carry your legacy, I'll honour your name,
In the dance of my life, I'll play your sweet game,
Though the world feels shattered, and the nights are so long,
I'll find you in whispers, in the notes of my song.

Six months today, and the tears still flow,
But I'll cherish your memory, let your love grow,
For in every heartbeat, in each breath I take,
You're the strength in my soul, the light that won't break.

Promise in the Ashes

On the day the world turned cold,
March's breath, a tale untold,
You slipped away, a whisper lost,
In shadows deep, I paid the cost.

In the grip of demons, I fought my fight,
Addiction's chains, a long, dark night,
But in that chaos, your voice rang clear,
A promise made, a vow sincere.

I stood amidst the wreckage, torn,
A heart once whole, now bruised and worn,
Your laughter echoed, a haunting sound,
In every corner where hope was drowned.

You were the light, my guiding star,
Now just a memory, a distant scar,
Yet in the depths of my despair,
I clung to dreams, to the love we shared.

Today I rise, a phoenix from ash,
With every step, I reclaim the past,
First place in hand, a bittersweet prize,
But all I crave are your proud, shining eyes.

Oh, how I long for your gentle embrace,
To feel your warmth, to see your face,
In every triumph, in every tear,
I search for you, I wish you were here.

I made you a promise, a solemn decree,
To rise from the darkness, to set myself free,
And though the world may never know,
In my heart, your spirit will always glow.

So here I stand, with a heart full of pain,
A testament to love, a dance in the rain,
For in every victory, in every fall,
I carry your memory, I carry it all.

And as the tears stream down my face,
I whisper your name, I seek your grace,
For in this moment, I hope you see,
I've kept my promise, I've set myself free.

Though you are gone, your love remains,
A haunting melody that soothes my pains,
And as I hold this trophy high,
I know you're proud, I know you're nigh.

In the silence, I hear you say,
"Keep fighting, my love, find your way,"
And though the ache may never cease,
In your memory, I find my peace.

The Fire Within

In the quiet corners of Tamworth's streets,
Where dreams are whispered, and hope retreats,
I stood, a trans man with a heart ablaze,
Sharing my goals, my vision, my ways.

But your smile, it faltered, a mask so thin,
A flicker of doubt, a whisper of sin,
You didn't believe, your eyes turned away,
As if my ambitions were meant to decay.

Yet, oh, my dear, your doubt is the spark,
That ignites the inferno, that lights up the dark.
For every "you can't," every scoff, every sneer,
Is fuel for the fire that burns bright and clear.

I am the master of this vessel I claim,
My body, my mind, I've forged in the flame.
I've danced with the demons, I've wrestled with pain,
In the depths of despair, I've learned to remain.

I've walked through the shadows, where few dare to tread,
Where hope is a whisper, and dreams lie for dead.
But I clawed my way back, with grit and with grace,
For I am the warrior who's found his own place.

You see, I've learned that the limits we bear,
Are chains of our making, a weight we must share.
To rise from the ashes, to shatter the mold,
To embrace the discomfort, to be brave and bold.

Each day is a battle, each moment a test,
To push past the pain, to strive for the best.
With discipline, dedication, I carve out my path,
With every step forward, I silence the wrath.

I've earned every inch of this body and soul,
Each scar tells a story, each wound makes me whole.
I've fought through the darkness, the fear and the dread,
And I'll stop when I stop, not when you've said.

So doubt me, if you must, but know this is true:
Your disbelief only strengthens the fire in me, too.
For I am the dreamer, the fighter, the light,
And I'll rise from the ashes, I'll soar to new heights.

So watch as I flourish, as I break through the night,
For the world may not see, but I am my own light.
In the heart of Tamworth, where dreams dare to grow,
I'll shatter the limits, and let my soul glow.

And when you look back, with your heart full of fear,
Remember this moment, remember me here.
For I am the master, the storm, and the calm,
And I'll rise from the shadows, forever my own balm.

In the Quiet of Your Care

In the quiet of my shattered mind,
Where shadows danced and hope was blind,
You found me lost, a whispering ghost,
A heart in pieces, a soul engrossed.

With gentle words, you wove a thread,
Through tangled thoughts, where I once fled,
You held my pain, a fragile glass,
And taught me how to let it pass.

Each tear I shed, you caught with grace,
A mirror held to my hidden face,
You saw the light beneath the scars,
And showed me how to reach for stars.

In the depths of despair, you stood so tall,
A lighthouse beacon when I would fall,
You painted colours on my grey,
And taught my heart to find its way.

With every session, you stitched my seams,
Revived my spirit, rekindled dreams,
You whispered strength when I felt weak,
And gave me words when I couldn't speak.

Now I walk a path once shrouded in night,
With courage blooming, a heart alight,
For in your care, I learned to see,
The beauty of the soul that's free.

So here's my heart, laid bare and true,
A testament of gratitude to you,
Dr Merima Isakovic, my guiding star,
You've changed my life, you've healed my scars.

In every breath, in every sigh,
Your wisdom lingers, it will not die,
For you've shown me love in its purest form,
A sanctuary found, a heart reborn.

To Rose,
My Guiding Light

In the quiet dawn, where dreams take flight,
You stood beside me, a beacon of light.
With every whisper, every gentle nudge,
You taught me to rise, to fight, to love.

Through sweat and struggle, through laughter and tears,
You held my hand, calmed my deepest fears.
In the mirror's reflection, I found more than form,
I found a spirit, a heart reborn.

You saw the potential buried deep inside,
A flicker of hope, a spark you'd ignite.
With every rep, every mile we'd chase,
You carved out my strength, my courage, my grace.

But it's not just the body, the muscles, the tone,
It's the bond that we forged, the love that we've grown.
In the darkest of moments, when shadows would creep,
You stood like a fortress, a promise to keep.

You taught me that friendship is more than a word,
It's the laughter we share, the silence unheard.
It's the way that you listen, the way that you care,
In a world full of chaos, you're always right there.

When I faltered and stumbled, you never let go,
You lifted me higher, you helped me to grow.
With every setback, you showed me the way,
To rise from the ashes, to seize every day.

Now I stand taller, with pride in my heart,
But it's you, dear Coach, who played the true part.
You've woven a tapestry of love and of trust,
In the fabric of my life, you are the must.

So here's to the moments, the lessons, the fight,
To the bond that we share, so pure and so bright.
In the echoes of laughter, in the tears that we've shed,
You've changed my whole world, you've filled me with love.

For the day will come when our paths may diverge,
But the love that you've given will always emerge.
In the depths of my soul, you'll forever reside,
My coach, my dear friend, my unwavering guide.

So thank you, dear Rose, for all that you've done,
For teaching me strength, for showing me fun.
In the journey of life, you've been my true star,
And I'll carry your light, no matter how far.

With tears in my eyes, I pen this refrain,
For the love that you've given, I'll never forget the pain.
You've shaped who I am, and I'll always hold dear,
The heart of my coach, my friend, my dear.

www.ingramcontent.com/pod-product-compliance
Lightning Source LLC
Chambersburg PA
CBHW061206070526
44583CB00025B/3131